Resurrecting Christianity

Restoring America's Soul

L. T. NIELSEN

ISBN: 0974586013
ISBN-13: 978-0974586014

DEDICATION

This book is dedicated to the memory of all those inspired men and women who were the founding fathers (and mothers) of this great nation. These were selfless individuals who pledged all they possessed, including their lives, their fortunes, and their sacred honor to establish a free Christian nation... a nation where God-fearing individuals could worship God and live according to their conscience. We are forever indebted to them.

They understood the subtle yet critical connection between morality and true freedom. They realized instinctively that for this nation to endure it would have to be built on a solid foundation of faith in Christ, utilizing the Ten Commandments as well as all the other teachings of the New Testament as its building blocks if it were to withstand the test of time.

For most of the 225 years since its inception, this "building" has stood strong... but today, liberals, socialists and those who mock traditional Christianity are destroying this once magnificent edifice. They're dismantling this God-inspired structure one brick at a time and it's fallen into a state of dilapidation that would render it almost unrecognizable to it's founders. It's riddled with the rot of racism, holes of hatred and the mounting mold of moral decadence. It's in dire need of a seismic upgrade and refurbishment.

We must begin immediately to shore up the sagging beams of liberty , replace the windows that have become stained with corruption, hypocrisy and political correctness, and replace them with new panes of honesty, openness and the light of truth. We need to peel off the countless layers of corruption, regulation and cronyism and lay down a fresh coat of freedom, fairness and common sense.

We're standing at a critical crossroads in our history, and unless we're able to make a much needed course correction, I fear that this once great structure may soon collapse and become a relic much like the Roman ruins.

However, there is hope! This grand old building can be restored to it's original luster. But the only way that's possible is for every person to take individual responsibility and personally make a commitment to return to the original principles of Christianity. This refurbishment will take some time... but we owe it to our founders to save their dream; we owe it to ourselves to preserve our freedoms, and we owe it to our children, to pass it on intact. This book attempts to explain how that can be done, and our individual responsibilities as we work at restoring America's soul.

CONTENTS

ACKNOWLEDGMENTS

I'd like to thank everyone who's had the courage to not only stand up and speak out for what's good and right with America, but also for those who've demonstrated even ***greater courage*** by pointing out what is ***wrong*** in our society, thereby opening themselves up for criticism and persecution. For much of the last four decades, this nation has been caught in a downward spiral, and religion and morality have been attacked and ridiculed as never before.

Many people, including some popular conservative talk-show hosts have demonstrated great courage as they've attempted to expose the press's liberal bias and hatred of people with traditional Christian values. And they've come to the defense of many people who've been the targets of attacks and even character assassination from the left. But now it's time for reinforcements.

And so I appeal to all citizens of Faith in America, no matter what your religious affiliation may be, to join this fight. The time has come for us to join forces as Christians, to fight side by side to restore the miracle that is **the United States of America.**

Thank you for your dedication to truth. May God grant us success as we join together with thousands of other Christian Soldiers in *our* moral responsibility... that of **Resurrecting Christianity, and Restoring America's Soul.**

CHAPTER ONE

THE STATE OF OUR NATION

In over two hundred years, there's not been a single nation or a coalition of nations powerful enough to destroy the United States of America. Whenever nations or enemies have tried, they've been repelled and defeated by brave patriots, utilizing all our recourses including the worlds most advanced technology to protect and defend our country, our government and our way of life.

And this nation has been able to remain free and strong for two reasons. First, because of the Spirit of the American people... people who have been and *still are* willing to give their lives in defense of God, family and country. But the second and even more important reason the United States has been able to withstand those who seek it's destruction, is because God has willed it to be so.

Corrupt nations and their leaders despise the United States of America. But God ordained this nation to be a bastion of hope, freedom and democracy in this world and they simply don't understand that. And we have risen as a result of our God-given rights, to be the most affluent, the most admired, and the most powerful nation this world has ever known.

If any foreign nation ever tried to shove down our throat their socialist or communist way of life, we would crush them. If some dictator attempted to curtail our religious liberties, or destroy the American dream, patriots from every corner of this great nation would spring to its defense and annihilate them without hesitation.

And yet... what the evil empires of the world have been unable to accomplish in the past 200 years is well on its way to becoming a reality. Not by foreign nations, evil dictators or Islamic terrorists who see us as the great Satan of the world, but by evil or at the very least, misguided individuals who live right here within our own borders! And our courts, our military, and our government have not only been protecting them as they destroy our freedoms, but in many ways are actually complicit in assisting them as they've methodically and purposely worked to quietly destroy this nation from within. And they're very close to winning this bloodless war !

Since January of 2009, we've sat around and watched as Obama and other radical liberals and leftists have carefully and quietly begun to dismantle this great nation. He's passed legislation and signed *executive orders by the tens of thousands* that are specifically designed to destroy the freedom and lifestyle that's been the envy of the free world for hundreds of years.

He's very close to accomplishing in a few short years what no foreign nation or military power has ever been able to do... and we've simply sat by and watched as he and his crony politicians have dismantled this nation one piece at a time. We're like a frog in pot of water that's slowly coming to a boil... too stupid to realize that the temperature is rising... and we're about to die.

If any foreign nation tried to impose these same restrictions and freedom-killing laws on us, we would have crushed them in a heartbeat!

Obama is destroying our economy, he's declared war on our energy industries, he's taken direct aim at Christianity, he's destroying capitalism, and he's worked tirelessly to apologize to the rest of the world for America's "exceptionalism" in an effort to force us to become just another second rate European style nation!

It's time to stop his treasonous agenda!

For whatever reason, this president is ashamed of our country! But this nation *is* still the greatest nation on Earth!

And it's not great because a hand full of Bible-thumpin' colonialists just happened to get lucky and take over a nation from a bunch of Indians who couldn't defend themselves.

It's not great because it just happens to have some of the best lands, climates and resources on the planet!

It's great because the God of Heaven ordained it to be so. It's great because it was founded by God-fearing men and women who God personally inspired and raised up specifically for that purpose. They understood, as we all must come to understand, that a nation without God can *never* truly be great.

Some have referred to the United States model of democracy and the U.S. Constitution as "the great experiment". Nothing could be further from the truth. God designed it, and God doesn't experiment... he already knows everything! And it's time we remember, reaffirm and recommit that "In God we Trust" is more than just a catchy phrase stamped on our currency.

The reason I've felt compelled to write this book is because I firmly believe that the number one issue facing America and threatening its very existence today isn't energy, it isn't the deficit, it isn't the Islamo-terrorists or even the Socialists who are currently in control of the White House.

The biggest problem and the most urgent threat to America today is the break-down of the American family which has been brought about largely by the expulsion of God from our homes, our hearts and from society!

One of the biggest problems facing "Christian America" today is the increasingly pervasive liberal notion that morality is relative and shifting. I assure you it's not! Peoples perceptions have changed, the meaning of words has morphed and become corrupt, but God never changes, and neither do his principles and commandments.

There are sincere individuals who believe that because times and attitudes and circumstances change, so too must morality... but that's another huge lie Satan would have us embrace. It's critical that honest thoughtful people understand and realize that the "new morality" of today isn't new at all... it's simply the "old immorality" of yesterday that's been given a more "politically correct non-judgmental" label. We must realize that God looks upon the perversions of today the same way he always has ever since the world began. *Morality isn't transient*. It's not subjective nor is it open to debate. (Intellectuals really hate that statement!)

The following declaration is critical to understand if we're to make any progress in restoring America to the spiritual status it enjoyed just a few short years ago. And many people may be offended by what I'm about to say... but if you consider yourself to be a **Christian**, this principle should be easy to grasp; and it's *very* important that serious Christians embrace it. It's simply this...

God <u>alone</u> defines what is "moral" and what is "immoral"; men and women have the opportunity to accept and obey God's standards of morality, or they may choose to ignore his standards and cast them aside. But our eternal destiny will ultimately be determined by whether or not we obey the commandments God gives us! In other words, it simply boils down to this...

Obey God's laws and be blessed, or ignore his laws, and deal with the consequences. It really is just that simple!

The ability to hold on to a principle and never waver from it no matter what the world might say or do is one of the most admirable traits of the Jewish nation. Although we as Christians believe the Jews missed the mark by not recognizing Jesus Christ as the Savior of the world when he came to earth on that Christmas night so long ago, we still respect the fact that these people have held fast to their beliefs and traditions for many millennia (except of course those who suffer from the disease of liberalism).

"Christians", therefore, could learn a lot from the Jewish people. We too must develop the courage and conviction to stay true to the teachings of Jesus Christ despite what the world believes, despite the pressures of society and public opinion, and despite what liberals, atheists or anyone else says or does. We must understand that the words Christ spoke, the things he taught some two thousand years ago, are just as true, just as relevant, and just as important for us today as they were when he taught them to his earliest followers.

We need to return to basic "Christian" values, the values Christ himself taught; the values the Bible continues to teach today.

I've spent many years in the construction industry. And one of the principles I learned about building is also an important principle of Christianity, and this is it...

If you want to build a structure that will forever be strong and stand the test of time, if you want an edifice that will be able to survive destruction from the elements and devastating forces of nature... you must begin by building on an absolutely rock-solid, reinforced, uncompromising foundation; because the safety and integrity of the entire structure and everyone and everything housed within its walls depends on it!

Christianity is no different. It's built on the foundation of Jesus Christ, his teachings, his commandments and doctrine. Christ's teachings are the foundational building blocks that we must build on today as well. Christ has given us commandments and shown us the right way to live. Everything necessary to find happiness in life *and in the eternities* has already been addressed and explained by Jesus Christ and was taught by his Apostles. And as "Christians" we have the obligation to build on that exact same foundation.

When we attempt to modify or ignore the things Christ taught, we remove the very blocks upon which Christ built his church, and the structure becomes the building of a man, not God. And when that happens, mark my word... the building will eventually come crashing down!

There's great danger in believing that because times change, values change as well... they don't. There's this notion that morality is old fashioned... it's not. There's a movement afoot by the liberal "elite" to try and convince everyone that we've outgrown God, that somehow we're too "sophisticated" to believe in "spiritual" things or that religion is simply a crutch for the "uneducated" and weak minded. Nothing could be further from the truth.

I hope that when you read this book, you won't be offended by what you read... at least not to the point of becoming defensive and hostile to its message. You see, one of the great things about a book is that it's impersonal by design, allowing you to read it then ponder and decide whether or not the message it sets forth is true. And paradoxically it's also very personal... because it *could* become your best friend as it causes you to recognize truth, re-evaluate your life, and implement needed personal changes.

And if you find it has merit, you needn't be offended or embarrassed by it... because no one needs to know. My hope is that you'll see the value of truth, and make the changes in your life that will bring the peace of God into your heart.

The reason for this book is to examine Christ's teachings to make sure that we as individuals and families build our "Christian Foundation" on those exact same building blocks Christ originally gave us.

I'm not suggesting that this country or this government should become our church, or that we give up our own personal religious affiliations. That's not what the founding fathers of this nation had in mind. What I am suggesting is that as *individuals*, we need to return to true Christian principles and strict adherence to Christ's original teachings. In doing so, we'll strengthen and keep free this nation that God established through inspired men and women, to be a light for all people, and a beacon of hope for the whole world to see.

CHAPTER TWO

"JESUS IS COMING... AND HE'S PISSED!"

That's what the bumper sticker read on the car in front of me as I was driving through Chico California in June of 1975. My first reaction was to cringe. It made me a little squeamish; after all, doesn't that sound a bit crass? Maybe a little irreverent? I mean... we're talking about Deity here! But the more I've thought about it, the more I've became convinced that that bumper sticker was actually right on target!

The thing is, those U.S. citizens who profess to be "Christians" make up the overwhelming majority of the population... about 75-80 percent by most estimates. The problem is that only a very small percentage of those who choose to identify themselves as "Christians" make any kind of serious effort to live the traditional, conservative "Christian" values Jesus taught in the Bible. Most Americans today simply don't accept or promote the values Christ taught! Why is that? After all, *isn't that the actual definition of a "Christian"?*

Does merely believing that there was once a man who lived and grew up in the vicinity of Jerusalem and called himself *Jesus* qualify a person to call themselves a Christian? If it does, then all the Jews, Muslims and even atheists can legitimately call themselves Christians! After all, most, if not all of these people also consider it a matter of historical record that a man known by that name lived and grew and started a religious movement near Jerusalem some 2000 years ago. They also accept that he was killed in that same vicinity by people who believed he was nothing more than a man. But that's just history... that's NOT the definition of a Christian!

To really be a "Christian" means we *literally* accept the idea that Christ was and is God, that he came to earth, took upon himself a body of flesh and bones, died on the cross for our sins, and was resurrected on the third day... and he did it for *all* of mankind because he loved us! He sacrificed his life so that one day we too could be resurrected, and be able to be washed clean by his blood, and then go on to live with him in a place much better than this place we currently call home.

But there are requirements of course, some "pre-requisites" to salvation that we need to understand and comply with. It isn't a free ride for anyone. If that *were* the case, there'd be no need for churches *or* the Bible. If Christian "salvation" didn't require any personal action or commitment on our part, then nothing we said or did would be of any consequence, hence nothing we said or did would either benefit *or* condemn us. But that's obviously not the case. Christ gave us a set of rules to live by... some requirements if you will, to prove to ourselves and demonstrate to Him and the world that we are, or one day will become fit to live with him again.

Christ taught the world many important "truths", and he explained why truth is important. Said he... ***"If ye continue in my***

***word, then are ye my disciples indeed, and ye shall know the truth,
and the truth shall make you free!"*** (St. John 8: 31, 32)

From this statement, it's obvious that there's a connection
between truth and freedom. Freedom is what America was
originally created for, and true Christianity *is* in a very real sense,
the embodiment of freedom.

You see, absolute freedom, without personal self-restraint or
moral social parameters to guide us is little more than anarchy and
chaos. In fact, there's no such thing as "absolute freedom"...that's a
paradox! True freedom ***demands*** discipline, and Christianity defines
correctly what the rules and standards of personal conduct must be
to enable us as individuals to understand and achieve our greatest
potential.

My dad put it this way... ***"You aren't free to do what you want
to do... you're only free to do what you ought to do."*** Think about
that... it's actually very astute.

Do you want to be truly free? Then you must have the courage
to accept the truth, even if it means that you'll very likely find
yourself standing alone at times among peers, friends... even
family. Do you have the courage to stand with Christ even when
your friends desert you? Remember, even Christ's closest
companions and confidants gave in to fear and social pressure and
turned their backs on him in his greatest hour of need, leaving him
to suffer alone.

To accept the truths Jesus taught in the Bible is never easy, but
God's promise to us all is that it will be worth it. And one of the
most important traits we'll ever develop in life is the ability to
recognize truth when we see it, and never confuse it with opinion,

bias or more importantly, political correctness which is rarely the repository of truth.

Individuals who are ignorant to or reject God's code of conduct, often say ridiculous things like... "Hey man, that's your truth, not mine!", or "Those are your morals, not mine!' This attitude not only reveals a certain animus towards God and religion in general, but demonstrates profound ignorance as it relates to "truth".

As Christians, we need to understand the importance of respecting every person's right to believe whatever it is they choose to believe. *Christ never forced his teachings on anyone*. But as Christians, we also have an obligation to make every effort to gently persuade people to come into the light, and bask in the warmth of absolute truth and love.

Truth is truth! It's not open to debate or legislation. People can certainly choose not to accept the truth, that's their right and I would never want to take that right away from them. But truth is independent of personal ideas or beliefs. Our responsibility is to seek out the truth and embrace it. Let me give you an example of what I mean.

Man CANNOT fly! Yes, I know he can with the help of some type of machine, an airplane, a hang-glider or whatever, but not without some type of external assistance. That is an absolute truth. There have been some people (usually under the influence of some mind altering substance) who have tried to disprove that fact, but more often than not, their attempts have met with injury or even death. Dropping like a rock does NOT qualify as flight.

Intelligent people recognize that statement as truth... Some people however choose to argue the point, but most of us don't take those kinds of people seriously anyway.

If you **happen** to be one of those people who wants to argue the point, then this book is probably not for you, and continuing to read further is only going to make you a little bit crazy.

If, however, you're the kind of person who loves truth, logic and common sense, read on! Together, I think we can come to an understanding of what truth really is, what a true Christian **should be**, and how truth is inseparably linked to peace and personal happiness.

Today we see certain groups or individuals in society who are becoming more militant, more aggressive, and more disrespectful of those who do have religious beliefs and convictions. These are people who will stop at nothing to destroy anyone or any thing they consider a threat to their life-style or personal liberal or secular agenda. They have increasingly become more and more intolerant of conservative Christians in America.

These are people who either despise or disbelieve in God. If they don't like the message you bring, or don't agree with the things you believe in, they'll go to whatever lengths necessary to see that you're destroyed. They'll use every means at their disposal to ruin you, your life, your reputation and your family. They especially love to attack Christian religions. And they'll make you pay for not going along with their liberal agenda. Our universities are littered with these individuals, masquerading as professors of "higher learning".

If you've ever had, or are in the process of cultivating the courage to stand up for true Christian values and Christ's teachings as contained in the Bible, I guarantee you already know, or will soon come to know the nasty venom these snakes can inflict. You'll learn first hand just how mean-spirited and vindictive these people can be. But you'll also learn for yourself the indescribable joy and satisfaction that comes from being on the Lord's side. You'll experience for yourself the promised "peace that passeth understanding" spoken of in the Bible. You can know for yourself the spiritual satisfaction reserved for individuals with true spiritual courage and commitment. We're not alone in this fight... remember Paul's words to the Romans... ***"If God be for us, who can be against us?"*** (Romans 8: 31)

Do you have the courage to be a "real, *true* Christian" in word and in deed? The decision is yours and yours alone to make. Just remember to seriously consider who it is you honestly wish to please, and who it is that will ultimately reward you for the choices you make in life.

CHAPTER THREE

CHRISTIANITY IS A VERB

Perhaps the biggest perversion of true Christianity over the years has come about as a result of uninspired, unconverted opportunists who skewed and corrupted the plain and simple gospel taught by Jesus Christ and purposely manipulate its message of hope and salvation to suit their own personal agendas.

Over the years, religious "holy men" intentionally corrupted the original teachings of the Gospel to make it more "palatable" to the average person, downplaying the necessity of **effort** and **lifestyle changes** that Jesus taught were necessary during his earthly ministry. They wanted to convince people that work, effort, commitment and sacrifice weren't necessary for salvation. They taught that the only service necessary was "lip-service". But that isn't what Christ or his Apostles taught.

The Gospel was never intended to be just an idea; it was intended to be a way of life.

When Christ called men to the ministry, they were expected not only to teach the things he taught, but live the way he lived. This meant being an example of the "believers", in word and deed.

Members of Christ's Church were expected to *live* the truths they taught. They were expected to keep the commandments, not just repeat them. They were expected to change their lives to conform to the teachings of this man we call Jesus.

Christ unequivocally clarified this concept when he voiced this warning found in the 7th chapter of Matthew, verses 21-23. Said he...

"Not every one that saith unto me, Lord, Lord, shall enter into the kingdom of heaven; but he that doeth the will of my Father which is in heaven.

"Many will say to me in that day,. Lord, Lord, have we not prophesied in thy name? and in thy name have cast out devils? and in thy name done many wonderful works?

"And then will I profess unto them, I never knew you: depart from me, ye that work iniquity."

Over the years, however, this concept has become lost in the minds of people, as many have been tricked into believing that all that's necessary is to simply "believe". Nothing could be further from the truth or a greater perversion of his doctrine.

When I say Christianity is a verb, what I'm saying is that God expects us to actually *live and do* the things we say we believe in. To say you believe in something, then refuse to actually do those things you claim to believe doesn't make you a "disciple", it makes you a "hypocrite", and Jesus was very critical of those he referred to as hypocrites. We've been instructed to be "doers of the word, and not hearers only, deceiving your own selves." (James 1:22) The notion that all we need to do is publically "confess" Jesus and then we're saved is simply a fairy tale. To believe that it doesn't matter what kinds of things we do, or what commandments we *intentionally* break because we've already been "saved" by a one time "confession" is of course nonsense. True Christians understand that belief or faith is important, even essential to salvation... but actual works, the demonstration and evidence of a person's faith is absolutely critical. The Apostle James put it best when he said...

What doth it profit, my brethren, though a man say he hath faith, and have not works? can faith save him?

If a brother or sister be naked, and destitute of daily food,

And one of you say unto them, Depart in peace, be ye warmed and filled; notwithstanding ye give them not those things which are needful to the body; what doth it profit?

Even so faith, if it hath not works, is dead, being alone.

Yea, a man may say. Thou hast faith, and I have works: shew me thy faith without thy works, and I will shew thee my faith by my works.

Thou believest that there is one God; thou doest well: the devils also believe, and tremble.

But wilt thou know, O vain man, that faith without works is dead? (James 2: 14 – 20)

Then he reminds us of the necessity of both faith and works when he powerfully put forth the following comparison...

For as the body without the spirit is dead, so faith without works is dead also. (James 2: 26)

It's *nice* to believe, but it's absolutely *critical* that we believe *and* act! That's why Christianity is a verb. You cannot call yourself a Christian unless you do as Christ taught. Christ's injunction to those who claimed to believe was... *"Come, follow me."* Those who become his followers must change their lives; the way they talk, the way they treat their neighbors, the way they live their lives. He expects us to become "New Creatures" as we put off the old ways.

Over time however, the necessity to "change" has been replaced by the rationalization that all a person needed to do was "confess Jesus", pay for absolution, and your money would buy back your soul and your good standing before God. This perversion of the word was popular with ancient priests mainly because it made them a good living and kept them in power. It became popular with the masses because it eliminated the effort God demanded of them to actually demonstrate personal worthiness. Jesus never intended for it to be so.

That's why we as "Christians" *must* return to the doctrines Jesus taught originally, and not be taken in by the religious "opinions" that characterize some of the churches we see around us today. I'm not inferring that all religions are bad or intentionally deceptive. I am saying that every "Christian" church should have as it's foundation, the principles and doctrine Jesus taught, and if a church can't justify it's teachings by comparing those teachings with the doctrines Christ taught originally... chances are they're simply teaching the "precepts of men".

Don't misunderstand what I'm saying here... it's Jesus alone who will save us... not our individual works... "lest any man boast". However, we must also actually "live" the commandments of God in order to demonstrate our faith... because faith *and* works as James taught, are <u>both</u> prerequisite to salvation.

CHAPTER FOUR

THE FORK IN THE ROAD

There are many beliefs which are commonly shared by Islam, Judaism and Christianity. All these religions accept as great Prophets, men such as Abraham, Isaac, Jacob, Moses and many other Prophets of the Old Testament. But there's a major fork in the road of religion that has and always will separate these religious camps one from the other. That "fork" is the man we call Jesus.

Christians generally accept Christ as the physical embodiment of Jehovah, the God of the Old Testament. They believe that he not only instituted Mosaic Law and established customs of sacrifice as types and shadows of his future sacrificial offering, but that he later died on the cross for all mankind, to answer the ends of the law and to complete or fulfill his law of sacrifice.

And having "fulfilled" the law, Christ did away with many of the outward ordinances and traditions of the Mosaic or lesser law.

Gone are the days of an eye for an eye, and a tooth for a tooth. The new or "Higher Law" requires followers of Christ to be forgiving, tolerant, willing to return good for evil, and love for anger.

Christ declared himself to be God incarnate and offered proof of that by coming back from the dead, showing his resurrected body to many, including the remaining eleven Apostles, the "Marys", and many others. This crowning miracle of resurrection was indisputable proof of his divinity and Godhood to those who knew and accepted him as God. So confident were his disciples that he was indeed the risen Lord, that they devoted the rest of their mortal lives to spreading his word and declaring to the world that he was the literal Son of God, the Redeemer of all mankind.

So you see, Christ is much more than just the greatest prophet who ever lived. He was and is God to all those who profess to be Christians.

So powerful were his teachings, so inspiring his life, that for thousands of years he's continued to change the lives of every person who accepts him as Savior and Redeemer of the world. As Christians, we believe and declare with boldness that he is precisely who he claimed to be.

But don't think for a moment that Christ expects you or me to blindly accept the word of Biblical writers or ancient historians when it comes to gaining a testimony of him. That's not the way testimony is received.

People can never discover God on their "own terms". All the study, historical evidences, archaeological findings and even the testimony of others, will not now, never have, and never will be able to *prove* to anyone that Jesus is the Christ.

God must either reveal himself to you, or he must forever remain unknown. We can only get to know God and begin to understand him if we seek for that knowledge in humility, and on His terms! And those terms are the very same for every human being.

Skeptics, unbelievers and secular progressives scoff at the notion of God "revealing" himself to anyone. And this skepticism, this arrogance, this doubt is precisely why they can never know him in their current state of mind. God doesn't reveal himself to the proud or the wicked. He doesn't acquiesce to "sign-seekers."

Now I'm not saying that all those who refuse to believe that Jesus Christ was and is God, are evil people. Generally, they're just ignorant and uninformed. The good news, however, is that they can come to know that Christ is God... if they're willing to put in the effort necessary to find out!

Let me also mention here, that there are many who openly declare that Jesus was a great prophet, a wonderful teacher or possibly a skilled "community organizer"... but they just can't accept him as being a "God".

If you happen to fall into that camp, then I suggest you haven't given serious thought to the subject. Either Christ IS God, as he declared himself to be or he is the biggest liar, the most evil imposter who ever lived! Possibly, as C. S. Lewis suggested, the Devil himself! Truth demands that he's either one or the other; either he IS God, or he's NOT... there's no middle ground possible, no wiggle room for sophisticated rationalization or personal interpretation. He never intended for there to be.

If you're not sure if Christ is who he says he is, and you truly want to know for yourself whether or not he is God, the Savior of the world, the rightful King who will one day return to reign on this Earth as King of kings and Lord of lords, there's an easy way to find out. It's simple actually. He made it simple so anyone could find out, and here's how you do it.

First, you must carefully read the Bible, (particularly the New Testament) study Jesus' teachings, trust in his words, repent of your sins, and then sincerely ask him in prayer if the things you've read are true. That's what the Bible teaches.

James taught us this simple formula for revelation in these words...

"If any of ye lack wisdom, let him ask of God, who giveth to all men liberally, and upbraideth not, and it shall be given him. But let him ask in faith, nothing wavering." (James 1: 5)

That's it! It's not brain surgery; it doesn't take a college education, it doesn't cost a single red cent, and the invitation to ask and receive an answer is open to every human being on earth. It makes NO difference to God whether you're black or white, bond or free, male or female, liberal or conservative, Christian or Jew. He will answer everyone who asks in sincerity.

So you see, this "fork" in the road, this "Jesus fork", is where we need to declare our allegiance and take a stand. Most of the world accepts him as just another prophet... but *serious* Christians know better. So make your choice, but choose wisely! It's not inconsequential like picking out a new pair of loafers. It's a little more important than that, and your decision will have serious and lasting consequences.

CHAPTER FIVE

THE "DUMBING-DOWN" OF CHRISTIANITY

It's disturbing to me when I talk to people who profess to be Christians, who *say* they believe in the Bible, but then arrogantly thumb their noses at virtually all of Christ's teachings. It's inconsistent and hypocritical!

When Christ "fulfilled" the law, he never said the Ten Commandments had been reduced to the Ten Suggestions! (At least I've never found that anywhere in holy writ!) And while he did do away with many of the harsher penalties of the Mosaic Law, he still expects us to keep all of the commandments to the best of our ability.

For example, we're no longer instructed to "stone" a person who gets caught committing adultery. However, we're still under strict command to never commit adultery! As a matter of fact, Christ went beyond the act itself and stated that any man who even "looked" upon a woman to "lust" after her, had already committed adultery with her in his heart. The bar has actually been raised, not lowered, to include an individual's thoughts! And more than just adultery is forbidden by Christ. Listen to what the Bible has to say...

"Know ye not that the unrighteous <u>shall not inherit the kingdom of God?</u> Be not deceived: neither fornicators, nor idolaters, nor adulterers, nor effeminate, nor abusers of themselves with mankind,

Nor thieves, nor covetous, nor drunkards, nor revilers, nor extortioners, shall inherit the kingdom of God."

(1st Corinthians 6: 9-10)

And that's just a partial list of things we've been commanded not to indulge in.

God gave us these teachings and commandments for a reason, and if we defy his teachings, it's considered very serious sin indeed, and will, if not repented of, keep us from entering Heaven's gate.

The big problem today is this: We live in a time of relative peace and prosperity, (at least for the moment) which unfortunately has always proven to be the perfect climate for spawning decadence, mischief and yes... liberalism. It's the ideal incubator for hatching permissiveness and perversion. When times are tough, people *naturally* turn to God for help and guidance. But when things are going well, we tend to forget God and look to each other for acceptance, pleasure, validation and self-gratification.

Look around yourself right now. You and I are seeing and hearing things on TV and radio that our parents would never have imagined possible just a few short years ago. Let me list just a few of the more obvious examples:

- Filth over the airways. Shock jocks who prey on the ugly dark side of human nature, including sexual exploitation, deviance and perversion intended to titillate their audience who can partake of this evil in the secrecy of their own home or vehicle. And they promote this vile trash all to gain "filthy lucre". (And then they seek to excuse this kind of filth under the pretense that what they're doing is actually a "legitimate art form"... but it's not, it's just filth.)

- SOB Laws, (Sexually Oriented Businesses) designed to make sexual perversion more readily accessible to everyone, *including our youth.*

- Corrupt laws and lawyers who care nothing for the soul of this nation, and only choose to worship at the alter of the "Almighty Buck"! These people often defend the "rights" of freaks and deviant groups such as NAMBLA, while actively fighting against traditional Christian values and principles.

- Pornography everywhere you look, degrading and destroying all that was once considered sacred and wholesome by our parents and grandparents. And this filth is defended, encouraged and propped up by left wing late night comedians who pander to the immoral masses.

- Television, news groups and entertainers everywhere pushing the envelope of decency further every day; actively encouraging everyone to not only accept, but actually embrace adultery, fornication, lying, cheating, and the homosexual agenda which is spreading like wildfire across America and around the world.

- Abortion with all it's ugly faces including the procedure from Hell known as "partial birth abortion". (AKA pre-delivery murder.)

These are just a few of the "symptoms" of a spiritually sick society. And like the proverbial "rotten apple in the barrel", if something isn't done to curb this rampant spiritual cancer, it will continue to spread rot and decay into every corner of society, destroying individuals, families and eventually our nation.

Can we really afford to turn a blind eye to this pervasive decadence? Are we truly Christians if we slink back into the shadows, not only covering the lamp of Christian faith with the basket of political correctness, but smothering the flame of faith beneath with fear of social repercussion?

My mother used to say to me... "If you don't stand for something, you'll fall for anything." That's the situation we find ourselves in today as a country.

Where do YOU stand? What path will YOU choose to follow? Will you have the courage to get off this hijacked P.C. bus that's headed down the road of rationalization and moral bankruptcy, or will you simply close your eyes, keep your mouth shut and hope for a non-fatal air-bag assisted collision?

It was Jesus who said... ***"Be ye either hot or cold, or I will spew thee out of my mouth."*** I interpret that to mean that he doesn't support or condone fence-sitters. As a matter of fact, I think he respects the evil person who at least has the courage to take a stand, more than he respects some jelly-spined fence-sitter who refuses to take a stand. It does make a difference in God's eyes whether we choose to follow him in word and deed, or simply *claim* to follow him yet never actually demonstrate it by our words and actions. ***Lip service alone will never get us inside the pearly gates.***

Christ **expects** us to take a stand... not just claim to be on his side. We must never forget... ***The road to hell is paved with good intentions... but, it's still hell when you finally get there!***

In years gone by, people weren't ashamed to be seen in church, or be seen praying to God or reading the Bible. Today, however, the media and the so called *"sophisticated intellectual elite"* look down on Christians as uneducated people who use religion as a "crutch".

And even those of us who know that Christ is real, and assert that religion isn't a crutch and claim we're *"not ashamed of the gospel of Christ"* find ourselves occasionally cowering beneath the gaze of the "elite" crowd because we don't want to be looked upon as freaks, or weirdo's, or someone who might be... shall we say... of "questionable intelligence".

Let's face it... being religious nowadays isn't really all that "popular" or easy.

An interesting thing happened to the people of the United States since the tragedy of 9-11.

On that fateful day in 2001, most of America had an instant attitude adjustment — a gut-check that I honestly thought would change the course of our nation for many years to come. But I was wrong. On that day, Christ became very important once again to most of Christian America, but in a matter of just a few short years, we observed the people of this nation push Christ out of their lives once again as we watched September 11 fade into the rear-view-mirror of history.

On that horrific day, time seemed to stand still for me. I'll bet it was much the same for you. Nothing seemed real. My wife frantically called and told me to hurry and turn on the radio - I did. I remember exactly where I was and exactly what I was doing at that moment.

I was stunned. I couldn't even carry on with my normal duties that day. I had to return home where I became uncontrollably riveted to the television.

What had just happened? How could this have happened in the United States of America? What was going to happen tomorrow or next week?

I watched David Letterman interviewing Dan Rather, and I saw him actually crying! Programs were changed; comedians lost their will to be funny. I wondered if it was the end of life as we knew it... would laughter and levity ever come back into our lives?

These were the thoughts and questions that crossed my mind and the minds of family and friends on that historic day. And the tragedy was even more punctuated in the intervening days as we watched with horror, the rescue efforts at ground zero, and realized that eerily, there were no passenger jets or private planes flying anywhere in the skies.

How was it possible that such a small group of evil fanatics could bring the mightiest nation on earth to its collective knees?

The following Sunday, churches were bulging at the seams. Suddenly it wasn't "weird" to go to church and listen to your minister. Suddenly it was "cool" once again for people to speak of God and pray for his protection... even in public!

And maybe the strangest sight of all was a news program showing the entire congress standing together on the front steps of the capitol, singing God Bless America in unison. In terms of miracles, I believe that had to be right up there with the parting of the Red Sea!

But, like the children of Israel, as soon as the immediate danger passed, the memories and nightmares quickly gave way to "business as usual". People quit going to church and life in America was back to "normal" once more. Before long, all the people who'd started wearing flag pins took them off, because some of the "elite sophisticates" began to criticize their "overt patriotism", calling it overbearing, offensive to "some people", and divisive in our "multi-cultural society".

Yep... that was just a few short years after the fact. How soon we forget.

Now more than a decade has passed and God and religion are just memories to many Americans. That "silly" reaction we had when we were traumatized on that horrific day so many years ago... was that simply a knee-jerk reaction? Probably... because now that we've had sufficient time to really examine what happened, we can look back more intelligently, more objectively, and realize that it probably wasn't all that traumatic or earth-shattering after all!

In fact, looking back on the whole twin-towers thing, I'm not so sure George W. Bush wasn't behind the whole thing! As a matter of fact, some "experts" claim that George W. Bush was probably just pissed off at Sadam Hussein and wanted to go to war because he wanted all their oil and he wanted to rule the world and ...

You see how easy it is for people to get crazy? That's how it works. People begin to rationalize, they start to speculate, they begin to doubt, they listen to whackos and their goofy conspiracy theories, and before you know it, they blame it all on the president for being such an "idiot!" (Never mind the fact that he has an I.Q. typical of doctors and surgeons. Never mind the fact that he got better grades in college than John Kerry! Never mind the fact that we never had another attack on our nation while Bush was the President!)

But, as they say on the left, "Don't confuse me with the facts, my mind is made up!"

I fear that people have simply decided we were just asleep or unlucky back in 2001, but now we've grown and advanced so much, that we're finally ready to move into the twenty first century by putting God on the back-burner once again, looking forward to more important things... like saving the planet!

Don't get me wrong... it's important to be good stewards of our planet. It's important to take care of mother earth and provide a better place for our children to live. But in doing so, our minds have been cleverly sidetracked once again, to focus on the physical, forgetting once again the spiritual which is infinitely more important!

And now we've been plunged into a world-wide financial crisis that's got everyone wondering what the fate of this nation and the entire world will be. **But the answer to our problems isn't financial... it's spiritual.** Without God, this nation has no future other than to follow all the other "has-been" nations into the ash-heap of history!

Such is the state of our nation. We've pushed God aside once more and we look to "man" to solve the problems we perceive to be the most urgent and pressing. The problem is, nothing is more pressing, more urgent, than strengthening this "Christian" nation morally and spiritually. Nothing is more critical to our nation's survival than putting the traditional family back in its rightful place as the preeminent social building block of society.

And a President who ran his campaign on "Hope" and "Unity" with "no more red or blue States... just purple"... proved to be the most divisive, the most racist , the biggest "divider-in-chief" this nation has ever known.

He ran on hope and change with a statement that if he didn't get the job done in his first term, that his Presidency would be a "one term proposition." Since then he's totally ignored the real problems facing this country, using most of his first term pandering to socialists, those on welfare, brain-dead college students and leftist radicals and environmental whackos. He's managed to divide nearly every group of people, and has insulted all serious thoughtful Christians as he's forced his anti-First Amendment agenda on everyone in the country. It's time for us to send him back home to Chicago to work on his future Obama Presidential Library plans.

CHAPTER SIX

DOG GIVEN PROBATION FOR ATTACK ON CAT!

It's absurd of course to even consider that this could be the headline of a newspaper in America... or is it? To think that an animal would be held criminally liable for any act against another animal is just ridiculous, since intelligent people understand that animals are just... well, animals! That's what animals do! (Except, of course in parts of Northern California where I've heard that some ill-mannered doggies have actually been arrested and charged with "doggie rape"... but... that's California...

Most people understand however that animals are just... well... animals, and are therefore not fettered or burdened with this pesky little thing we call "conscience" or "moral compass."

There's a good reason for that too, and that reason is really very simple. Human beings are the offspring of God...animals are not.

Animals are the creation of, NOT the offspring of deity, and as such, they have not inherited nor can they acquire the same intelligence or moral compass humans naturally possess.

As God's children, we're endowed with many of the same characteristics and attributes of God. We look very similar (Christ appeared after his resurrection like other men physically. John declared that when Christ appeared again, that "...we would be like him, for we shall see him as he is." *1 John: 3:2*) And we are all born into this world with an inner moral compass that if cultivated and encouraged to grow, becomes what we often refer to as "conscience." It's that little inner voice that tells us instinctively whether or not something is right or wrong, good or evil.

Some argue that these aren't God-given traits at all, but learned responses. But those who argue this, I believe, are either ignorant, intentional liars or have allowed themselves to be deceived. They reject these feelings and deny the deity connection to justify or rationalize their own inappropriate behaviors despite the guilt they often feel. (Which by the way is evidence of a conscience.)

Certainly our surroundings influence us greatly, but even people who are brought up in the most basic and primitive of cultures have demonstrated this curious phenomenon we recognize as "conscience" when they commit horrific crimes such as murder or rape. Even with no laws, they instinctively try to commit these acts in secret, away from the view of others so as not to "get caught". Once they've committed such a crime, the perpetrator feels guilt, fear, remorse or whatever else you want to call it, and they seek to cover it up. That's what a guilty conscience does.

Animals, on the other hand, will kill each other or their prey out in full view of "society", and never worry for one moment that someone might see them do it, nor do they feel any remorse afterwards for those actions.

The point I'm trying to make here is that humans are not animals, and because we're not, we must not act like animals. God expects us to live on a higher plane than the brute beast.

As children of God, we also have this inner voice that strongly speaks to us of the reality of life AFTER this life; a place where death will have no more power over us once we are resurrected; a place where we will have to answer to a "higher being" for our actions while on Earth. And this powerful belief is not unique to Christians. Nearly ALL religions believe in this doctrine in one form or another.

Even the vilest militant Islamic radicals (who have this crazy notion that if they can kill as many innocent people as possible while acting as human explosive devices) *believe* that Allah will somehow be so pleased with their "heroic act" that he will reward them on the other side with 72 virgins!

The truth of course is that they just end up going to hell regardless of what they've been brainwashed to believe because that's where God sends *all* murderers!

Men and women are on this earth because God placed us here. It was He who created this planet for his children to dwell on, and as children, we're expected to live life on a higher plane than the animals do.

If there was no such thing as God, there would be no such thing as right or wrong. Animals don't live their lives or raise their offspring a particular way because they're guided by conscience or values. They're simply driven by instinct, survival of the fittest.

Man on the other hand has a conscience. Men and women have this spark of divinity that instinctively causes them to care about the welfare of others. Good people seek out the weak, and often go to great lengths to help them. These actions are unlike animals who naturally try to kill off the weak, demonstrating natures principle of the survival of the fittest. But as human beings, we are so much more than just animals. And God expects us to act like it!

So let's examine the laws of God as well as a few of the inspired writings of the United States constitution. These documents ought to act as guide-posts for us as "Christian Americans". True thoughtful Christians would never have a problem gleaning understanding and enlightenment from such documents as...

- The Ten Commandments.

- Christ's teachings during his earthly ministry.

- The principles embodied in the U. S. Constitution and it's amendments.

So let's briefly examine these one at a time to see how TRUE Christian Americans should conduct their lives, and see how we measure up individually and as a nation.

CHAPTER SEVEN

THE TEN COMMANDMENTS

The Ten Commandments have been defined and accepted by billions of Christians throughout the ages as Gods moral code for man to live by. I want to address this concept just for a moment because I also know, as previously mentioned, that there are many individuals who, when they hear the word "moral", immediately get defensive and argue that morality is relative, that no one should try to "shove their morals down other people's throats"!

First of all, let's be real clear about this most basic Christian principle. When we speak of morals, we're obviously speaking of **Gods morals**, or the boundaries God has set regarding the social interaction and conduct of the human race. These boundaries are defined in biblical doctrine.

The first thing we need to understand and accept if we're to have any intelligent conversation is that ***God establishes morality, not man.*** If God says something is right to do, then <u>it is right</u> to do. If he says a particular thing is wrong to do, then <u>it's wrong</u>. And it may not always appear black and white to everyone. But even if it seems inconsistent at times, there's always a logical reason for it. For example...

God declared... "Thou shalt not kill". Yet, there are multiple instances in the Bible where God clearly commanded men to kill. Now, an intelligent person will readily understand that what God was actually saying was... thou shalt not "murder". God expects us to defend our homes, our families and our country even to the shedding of blood. There's a huge difference between "killing" and "murdering".

Plants and animals on the other hand have no morals. Therefore, if a plant or an animal kills something, it's not "immoral"... it's just nature, or natural.

Morality only applies to the human race, but *as* humans, **we do not get to vote on what morality is.** Many people debate it, some choose to ignore it, but in the end, God will demand an accounting of each of us for our compliance or rejection of it.

I imagine that if you're a Christian, and you accept the Bible as God's word, you won't have a big problem with the things I've just said. If you're not a Christian, probably nothing I say will make any sense to you, and it doesn't really matter because this book is clearly intended for those professing and desiring to be "practicing" Christians.

There's one more fact I feel I should point out and remind everyone of before getting into the real meat of this book... and it's simply this...

NO ONE IS PERFECT, AND GOD DOESN'T EXPECT PERFECTION FROM US! ONLY JESUS CHRIST WAS PERFECT!

We ALL sin and WE ALL fall short of the "glory" of God!

Therefore no one is justified in believing that their "pet sins" are more or less serious than the "pet sins" of any other individual!

Let me try to illustrate this principle better by using the following example. It's from an article titled "Just Fill in the Blanks".

"Hi... my name is Bob. I consider myself to be a good Christian, and I know that generally means I should adhere to a particular set of beliefs and conform to certain accepted standards as outlined in the Bible. But you see... it's not that easy for me, because I happen to be _____. (Just fill in the blanks) I didn't want to be... I mean, I never actually sat down one day and decided I wanted to be this way. Nor did I just wake up one day and "discover" that I was _____ Hey... it's just natural for me! It's who I am! I was born this way. The thing is... just because I have this uncontrollable urge to be _____ doesn't mean I should be ashamed of it... right? And since I was born this way, there's nothing I can do to change it, and society shouldn't expect me to. So don't ask me to change... just accept me as I am because I'm not about to change for you or anyone else!"

This logic is suitable for any and all situations you may find yourself in. This will undoubtedly apply to one of your own character "traits" so just fill in the blanks with whatever best describes you. And don't worry about what people might think... in this day and age, no one's going to judge you for what you do or how you act. It's not P.C. to be "judgmental" and the media loves to crucify, belittle and mock those "holier-than-thou" nut-cakes who have the audacity to profess a belief in God or actually take a stand regarding what's "right" or "wrong", "moral" or "immoral"! So... what'll it be? Just fill in the blanks. Here's a list that may help you identify your own personal character "trait"...

A. an adulterer

B. a fornicator

C. a cheater

D. a pedophile

E. a liar

F. a thief

G. an embezzler

H. a stalker

I. a homosexual

J. a voyeur

K. an alcoholic

L. a bully

M. a druggie

N. a murderer

0. a rapist

P. a womanizer

Q. a Sabbath breaker

R. a hypocrite

S. a gossiper

T. a lawyer

Ok... I was just kidding around with that lawyer thing, but the point is this: Every person has something in his or her life, some "chink" in their armor they have to deal with. But it's these differences and a thousand others that make us unique as individuals. Every living person has demons to fight. But character is formed and wisdom built by recognizing, fighting and conquering the personal battles that are waged within the recesses of our own souls... **and it was never intended to be easy.** Yet with effort and persistence eventually we can conquer and overcome any of these destructive "traits". **The notion that simply because something is natural, and therefore it ought to be accepted by ourselves and society is of course patently ridiculous!**

Every person born into this world has natural sinful tendencies they have are required to deal with. It has to do with this concept we often refer to as "fallen man" or "original sin". But God expects us to identify, control and overcome every evil (or natural) tendency. So let's be real clear about one thing:

These "natural" desires in and of themselves, do NOT make a person "evil"! On the contrary, they just makes us "human"... like everyone else. And ALL of us have issues with one or more tendencies from the list above. The difference between success and failure when it comes to character and integrity in life is not IF we happen to have any of these "tendencies"... but whether or not we choose to embrace and "act out" on them. Or will we obey God and *make the effort He expects us to make, to "suppress" these tendencies and learn how to "overcome" them? The question is, are we willing to fight these natural urges in an effort to build character, and develop self control as God requires?*

Often times, "well intentioned" individuals, whether family or friends will seek to excuse and even enable those who might be struggling with any of these moral issues. But they are NOT helping them by joining the chorus of P.C. activists prodding them on and assisting them with a plethora of enabling rationalizations! On the contrary, they're simply throwing them under the bus, caving in to politically correct ill conceived excuses that are actually destroying the souls of these individuals and, fracturing the moral foundation of our communities and our nation.

Those who reject God's laws, and choose to climb on the P.C. bandwagon of Liberal Secularism and moral apathy absolutely have the right to make that choice... and I will stand with them and defend their right to make that choice! But as their brother and one who loves them, I feel obligated to remind them they'll have no excuse and no right to complain that God "wasn't fair" when He "rewards" them for those wrong choices. (End of article)

Now, if you happen to struggle with any of the aforementioned issues, don't be offended, and don't get defensive... because you're actually pretty normal. And please, don't condemn those who do struggle with things that don't happen to be an issue or a temptation for you. Just remember, we all have issues, even if they weren't identified specifically in the list above, and any of these "flaws", left un-corrected and un-repented of, will destroy a person and keep them from entrance into the Kingdom of God.

There's a poem that illustrates this point very well... it was penned by Ella Wheeler Wilcox. It goes like this...

"It's easy enough to be virtuous

When nothing tempts you to stray;

When without or within no voice of sin

Is luring your soul away.

But it's only a negative virtue

Until it's been tried by fire.

And the soul that is worth the treasures of the earth

Is the soul that resists desire."

Understand this! We all struggle with "unholy desires", but conquering those desires is what makes people great. It's what builds character!

At this point, I feel the need to explain in simple terms, "natures" rational and the "logical" argument why it just makes good sense not only to accept these truths, but why it's important from a practical standpoint to fully embrace God's rules of morality as it relates to society.

First, let's take a careful look at the previous list of "sins" and as we review them, ask yourself this question... *"If everyone in the world embraced or implemented these "choices", what would be the result? And, would the world be better off or worse off as a result of embracing these negative "traits"?"*

To help understand the ramifications of each "choice", let's look at these issues one at a time...

- **Adultery**... The single most important unit in every society is the family. Destroying a home, tearing parents apart, and fracturing the lives of children are among the most evil acts that can be perpetrated by any individual. And that is exactly what adultery does. It destroys the marriage relationship, shatters homes, wrecks families, and extinguishes love and trust. So ask yourself the question... WWHIEDI? (What would happen if everyone did it?)

- **Fornication**... The most sacred, special and uniquely personal gift any human being can give to the person they love and intend to marry, is the gift of self. And this gift is so much more sacred and special when that person has saved him or herself sexually as well... (which is exactly what Christ has commanded and expects each of us to do.) So ask yourself *the* "question" as it relates to fornication.
Understanding that fornication is a serious sin, realizing that the fruits of this inappropriate act are suspicion, STD's, regret, guilt, distrust and children being born out of wedlock, ask yourself the question... WWHIEDI?

- **Cheating**... Cheating has many faces and definitions. There are many ways to cheat. But all forms of cheating are dishonest, destructive, and offensive to God. Whether it's cheating on your spouse, your employer, your taxes or your schoolwork... it's dishonest and spiritually damaging. Again, ask yourself... WWHIEDI. You're probably starting to notice a pattern developing here. It's no surprise that all these things have a very negative impact on society and on individuals. Yet all of us have one or more of these natural "tendencies" we have to deal with. The fact that they're "natural", however, does NOT mean they should be tolerated by ourselves and they should certainly never be embraced! To the contrary... these flawed character traits should and must be overcome in order to develop character, strengthen individuals and families, keep society healthy and prepare ourselves to return to live with God.

• **Pedophilia**... This "defect" in character is obviously one of the vilest and disgusting flaws known to man. Those who engage in this evil activity destroy lives, not just the lives of their victims, but family, loved ones and future generations yet unborn. One would think that disdain and even hatred for this practice would be universal, yet there are many who actually defend this perversion. Organizations such as NAMBLA openly fight for their "rights" to be perverts. This practice is so repugnant it doesn't merit further discussion.

• **Lying**... Honesty and trust are crucial to every relationship. Not just personal relationships, but also the relationship that exists between employer and employees, clergy and parishioners, government and citizens, teacher and students. People are only as good as their word. If people were 100% honest in all their dealings, nearly all our laws could be eliminated. Police, lawyers and judges would rarely be called on. Jails and prisons could virtually be eliminated. So *honestly* ask *yourself* this question... "'If every person in the world was as honest as I am, what kind of world would this be?" If the answer is that it would be a great world, congratulations! If the answer is anything less than that... perhaps there's some work to be done.

• **Stealing**... There are few things that make a person feel more angry, more violated and more helpless than when some thief breaks into their home, car, or place of business, and takes what they've worked so hard to acquire. Thieves are the scum of the earth, parasites on society. So when you ask the question, WWHIEDE, the answer should be obvious. It would create absolute anarchy! And murder, destruction and chaos would be the ultimate result. No society can survive or thrive if they don't agree on these important social values.

• **Embezzlement**... This is another ugly sibling to lying and thievery. Obviously if everyone participated in this, there would be anger, suspicion, treachery, and a general breakdown of society.

• **Stalking**... Stalkers are predators that need to be dealt with by the law. Every person is entitled to their own privacy, and that privacy needs to be respected by everyone. But those who have a sick pre-occupation with an individual who wants nothing to do with them are essentially forcing on someone that which they have no right to do. No person would want someone stalking them, but many people forget to practice the "golden rule".

• **Homosexuality**... There's a reason why this particular act is referred to in the Bible as the "sin against nature" or as the Bible also labels it..."unnatural". And the reason is obvious. First, those who give in to these desires *and embrace them*, do so to the dishonor of all their ancestors who sacrificed so much throughout the centuries to make it possible for them to come into this world. By their "choice", their pedigree line is simply terminated and erased. And the result of their selfish "desires", is to effectively destroy the noble efforts of all their progenitors. They do not pass on to children the gifts, talents and DNA that managed to survive through the centuries. Instead, they effectively end their genetic participation in the human race. (Unless of course they institute a surrogate "breeding program" to fulfill their desires to be a "parent". But God is surely offended by that kind of perverse thinking.) If everyone embraced the act of homosexuality, the entire human race would cease to exist inside of one or two generations. It's very easy to see why this defect is so horribly wrong simply from a biological standpoint.

• **Voyeurism**... There's no serious person who would debate the impropriety of being a peeping-tom. Yet there are many people who are caught up with this sick obsession. Like all destructive flaws, this "urge" needs to be suppressed and mastered. Voyeurism never ends well, yet many people fantasize about this activity. Hollywood and independent movie-makers understand this sick fascination, and actually rely on it to make themselves rich. People often get a similar exhilaration attending a porn flick as they do when they act out their voyeuristic tendencies. And as long as there are people willing to sell their souls for cash, there will be perverts ready and willing to act as money collectors for these misguided individuals.

• **Alcoholics**... Alcoholism is a disease that has one distinct advantage over most other "diseases". <u>If you never try it, you can never catch it</u>. I've had numerous conversations with drunks in my lifetime, but I've never caught their "disease". We need to rely on parents first and foremost, to help children avoid this destructive activity. We need to help people understand that having complete control of your mental faculties is always the best way to really enjoy life. Sure, we laugh at some of the ridiculous things "drunks" do, but in reality', it's no laughing matter. Thousands of young people loose their lives each year because the media makes it look like drinking is somehow a positive social activity. It's not. Imagine how horrible this world would be if everyone was an alcoholic. I don't believe I need to elaborate on this flaw any further.

• **Bullying**... Bullying has always been around. Some claim that with the advent of the internet, it's much more difficult to deal with now than it was in the past. There's certainly some truth to that. However, many of our young kids are being bullied and harassed and can't deal with it because their parents simply haven't taught them Christian values.

If a child doesn't understand their true relationship to God, problems become much more difficult to deal with. When parents don't have a personal relationship with God, it's much more difficult to give guidance to children to help them cope with ridicule. No one should feel alone here on earth. And God intended for loving parents to be the primary teachers in every home, to love, encourage and counsel their children as they go through difficult times. *But trials are actually a natural and very important part of human life.*

If parents had a sound Christian foundation, and actually taught their children the "Golden Rule" while their children were young, most bullying would simply be eliminated. Also, people who are grounded in faith understand that *life isn't fair* and sometimes we need to look to others for help and healing. Sometimes, we need to look to God.

• **Drugs**... Drug dealers are to the physical side of life what pornographic movie-makers are to the spiritual side of life. Both are despicable, because all their efforts are focused solely on making money, *knowing* they're destroying the lives and souls of individuals *and their families*. But to these evil people, the "almighty buck" or as Christ called it, "filthy lucre" is the only thing that has real value in their pathetic lives. Make no mistake about it... these people will answer to God for their sins.

• **Murder**... This act is so despicable, so obviously evil, it requires no further elaboration.

• **Rape**... No one with any degree of honor or conscience needs to be convinced that this is one of the most horrible, disgusting perversions know to man. One of the things that makes it so despicable is the fact that when one person uses force to take that which is so personal, so private, so sacred and does it against the will of another, they are violating that which is most sacred to all of us... our will. Our will is the only thing we truly own, and when someone violates it, they truly are the most vile of all creatures.

• **Womanizer**... God has declared that man and woman should marry... and the two should become "one flesh". This declaration means more than just the fact that they become one "entity"... it also means that they're off limits and out of play when it comes to members of the opposite sex. Men or women who continue to flirt, date, seduce or seek out emotional responses from other individuals after they have already tied the knot with their "mate" are doing things which are *inappropriate under any circumstance*. Obviously, this type of behavior is destructive to a marriage relationship, since it erodes trust, destroys homes and families, and breaks up the most sacred relationship known to man, which is of course marriage. Again, ask yourself WWHIEDI?

• **Keeping the Sabbath** ... God knew our lives would be filled with stress, worries, and the necessity to work in order to survive. He realized people would need a time to rest, to unwind, to build family and other healthy social relationships as well as draw nearer to him. That's why he established the Sabbath day. It was clearly made to be a help and a blessing to mankind. Yet we've decided that it's really not a day of rest at all, but a day of "recreation"... and most of us are just as, if not more busy on that day than any other day. The problem is, it really doesn't benefit us spiritually if we simply change our activities, and not our attitudes. If each of us would take the time to unwind, to be of service to others, to worship God and strengthen our family relationships, this country would be a much better place for everyone.

• **Hypocrisy** ... It's interesting that hypocrites were some of the people Jesus routinely targeted as those he least approved of. Nobody likes a hypocrite. To declare that one *ought* to act in a particular way, then *intentionally* act just the opposite, is the personification of dishonesty. And hypocrisy is a very close relative to political correctness. You see, people are politically correct, not because they actually believe a thing to be right or wrong, but because they don't want to be "perceived" as one who is "intolerant" or "judgmental". Not only that, they often use political correctness to denigrate their opponents, while embracing within themselves the exact same traits they publicly condemn. "Hypocrites" and the "politically correct" are paternal twins.

• **Gossip** ... Gossip is actually quite closely related to hypocrisy as well. It's words spoken about others which are generally unkind, and usually spoken by those who don't have the courage to say those same things in the presence of the person they're demeaning. Often, those things said during a "gossip session" are not just unkind, but untrue as well. And although many times there is a thread of truth woven into the fabric of the conversation, half-truths often end up being the most damaging kind of lies. The best rule of thumb to follow is the rule my mom taught me when I was small... "If you can't say something nice, don't say anything at all!"

God has denounced ALL these activities and more, and scripture is unambiguous on all these issues... so the choice is simple. Obey God and be blessed... or disobey God, and take your chances. It really is just that simple! *Voluntary, conscious participation in any or all of these sins will ultimately net the same results, which renders it pointless to try to list these sins in any particular order of severity.*

God has declared plainly that *no unclean thing can enter into the Kingdom of Christ...* (Ephesians 5:5) so the ultimate end will be that by participating in any of these sins, we *personally and consciously* make the choice that we're not interested in achieving, receiving or becoming all that God wants for us. We *are* responsible for our own fate, which includes banishment from God's Kingdom unless we conform to HIS will. So choose your path... it's your decision. But please, can we just quit campaigning and focusing on those groups or individuals who have managed to convince society that their "tendencies" are somehow more "worthy" of our sympathies and acceptance.

By utilizing political correctness and character assassination, some groups have been very successful at "legitimizing" their own flawed tendencies, and have successfully convinced the masses that their "tendencies" should be tolerated and embraced by all of society! But truth will never change despite social pressure or "accepted lifestyles" and man cannot and never will be able to convince God to change his doctrine or his principles.

God has denounced ALL sexual activity outside the bonds of marriage! PERIOD! End of story... no exceptions! That includes adulterers, fornicators, (which unfortunately has come to include nearly ALL Americans) as well as every other "unholy" sexual relationship or activity. **God expects those who profess discipleship to adhere to his commandments regardless of what the world thinks, says, or does.**

Human beings do not have the ability nor the power to pressure God into modifying the standards He's established for admittance into Heaven. And he's certainly not going to abolish morality simply because a bunch of whiners think it ought to be that way! *God's not interested in nor is he swayed by popular sentiment, judicial mandate, political correctness or currently accepted social standards!* The good news is that God wants all of us to find happiness, but that can only be done by obeying his laws.

So, with that in mind, let's proceed with a brief but valuable examination of the Ten Commandments, and see why God expects each of us to comply with these "laws of happiness".

Number One

Thou shalt have no other Gods before me.

The Bible teaches us that God is a jealous God. A God who's given us everything... food, water, a climate favorable to our existence, (despite what global warming activist say) as well as intelligence and the ability to think and improve our circumstances.

All he asks in return is that we acknowledge him as the giver and creator of life, honor his wishes and make a *serious* attempt to keep his commandments; which by the way, if we do, he blesses us immediately with more blessings and rewards.

Atheists, secular progressives and many liberals try to debunk the idea of God, because it stifles their agenda. They hate the very concept of God because if there really is a God, that would make them "inferior" to another being, and they simply cannot admit that anyone or anything could be superior to themselves. These are the people the scriptures aptly describe as "haughty, proud and stiff-necked."

They often argue there's no such thing as God, trying to persuade as many as possible to follow their heathen ways and become godless like themselves. Many of these "unbelievers" however change their tune and develop a belief in God as they grow older and acquire wisdom and experience. Most of the "hold-outs" will have a change of heart about two minutes before they suck their last dying breath; **everyone else will follow suit immediately after that... I guarantee it!**

Number Two

Thou shall not make unto thee any graven image.

A graven image is anything man-made in our lives that deflects our attention from, or demands homage be paid to something OTHER than the true and living God.

For some, it's been and often still is a statue, made of wood or stone; lifeless figures that men pray to in place of the "living" God, hoping that this "object" or the person or the thing this object represents, will somehow make intersession with God for and in their behalf. To Christians, however, this is an absurd notion since

Christ taught that He is the great "mediator", and that "No man cometh unto the Father, but by me." Christ alone is our salvation, and we can only approach the Father through Him! Not some statue or golden calf or lifeless idol.

But it's really more that just that. Today we too often find the object of our adoration, our "substitute" for worship on the Sabbath day, not in the form of a man or beast, but in the form of the "arena". Football, soccer, baseball, hockey, basketball, a rock concert, a Broadway play or the race track, all deflect our attention from the God who gave us life, to the man-made temples of entertainment and social worship which can only leave us empty and unfulfilled in the end.

The underlying reason for pushing God aside and replacing him with other diversions on the Sabbath day is pride and our obsession with entertainment, personal gratification, and the "Almighty Buck". Money has become God to many of us and we often find it very easy to rationalize our worldly desires and cravings, relegating our actual days of worshiping God to Easter and Christmas.

Another really sad commentary on society today is the belief that if a "practicing Christian" does choose to attend church on a weekly basis, there must be something wrong with them. They're regarded as "prudish" or "fanatical".

What are we thinking? Shouldn't we ALL at least make the effort to worship and pay tribute to the God we profess to believe in? Isn't that what "true Christians" do?

I noticed a billboard one day outside a church which read... "Seven days without God, makes one weak." An astute observation. We all need God in our lives, to elevate and lift our spirits and give us the desires to become better.

Number Three

Thou shall not take the name of the Lord thy God in vain.

This is number three on God's "thou shalt not" list, yet men and women, apparently as a display of arrogance or disdain for Deity, choose to defy this commandment regularly with wanton disregard for the feelings of sincere believers. Hello! It's number three for a reason!

I've found that in general, people who take God's name in vain, (including the common, careless casual use of Christ's name) are people who are simply shallow thinkers. They don't take God seriously and they demonstrate this by thumbing their nose at this commandment as if it's just nonsense! As true Christians, we ought to know better and we ought to take a stance against it!

But taking God's name in vain isn't just the usual thoughtless and offensive "G_ _ D_ _ _" outbursts of the un-religious or the disrespectful; it actually goes way beyond that.

Taking God's name in vain also includes the hundreds, even thousands of charlatans and scammers who have figured out that they can manipulate the minds of honest humble God-fearing people into giving them their hard earned money, all in the name of charity, goodness, God and religion.

These are scammers and predators of the worst ilk. I'm speaking of televangelists and preachers who in an effort to get

YOUR hard earned money, tell heart-rending stories of the poor, the needy, the orphans in "Wamba Tamba" or some other far off village in some third-world country, who need YOUR money in order to survive! They sometimes evoke real tears from their followers as they show photos of helpless children wallowing in filth with protruding bellies and tear-stained faces.

One in a hundred might... *might* actually donate some of the proceeds of these infomercials to help out these little children somewhere in the world, but for the most part, *nearly all the money collected by these TV "ministers" goes to pay for expensive programming, production staff, studios, advertising, opulent sanctuaries, staff and office equipment, expensive cars, country club fees, nice suits and furniture for these "preachers" and for their palatial mansions.* (Have you seen some of the mansions these guys live in?) And... *if* after all these "necessary" expenditures are taken care of and there's anything left in their coffers, they **might** just send a little something off to the orphans.

I actually witnessed a preacher plead with destitute widows, to send in their "love offerings", even though they apparently didn't have the money to do so. "Just put it on your credit card" he shouted, "and God will bless you for your demonstration of love, faith and Godly compassion!" Really?

The truth is, most of these so-called TV "preachers" who run around in fancy suits, drive expensive cars, live in beautiful mansions and solicit money every day of the week, are nothing but scammers taking advantage of innocent God-fearing people who honestly *do* want to help God's children; and those individuals who do sincerely make contributions believing that they're helping the poor will undoubtedly be rewarded for making an honest effort to assist in God's work.

Many of these slick televangelists however could care less about the poor. To them, it's all about the almighty buck!

I watched a documentary on cable detailing several of the more successful "ministries" and how much of each dollar actually got sent to help the poor. In their examples, less than 13 cents in a dollar ever made it to those in need. And those were considered the "legitimate" ones.

Make no mistake about it... scamming people to get their money for personal gratification, while invoking the name of God, is just as bad and possibly even worse than simply verbally taking God's name in vain! These "ministers" who rob the poor in order to line their own pockets will surely inherit the same rewards as all the other liars and thieves.

I'm not saying there aren't some honest people or organizations that actually DO "do good" in the name of religion. There are many preachers and ministers who love God and try their best to do his work. What I am saying is this... please, do your homework.

There's nothing positive, virtuous, or admirable about throwing your money at someone who's pocketing the lions' share of your hard earned cash for his or her personal gratification. If it somehow makes you feel better to throw your money at that kind of person, then go ahead and do it. Just a word of caution... I'm not convinced that God rewards people for stupidity, no matter how sincere that stupidity might be!

If your minister is constantly harping on donations, driving around in luxury sedans and living in a home that's much nicer than most of the homes his parishioners live in, chances are he's in it for the money, and not for the glory of God.

Bottom line... check out your "gifts" to see where all that money is actually going.

Number Four

Remember the Sabbath day, to keep it Holy.

An entire book could be devoted to this single commandment alone. Suffice it to say that this has become one of the big ten which is not only summarily dismissed, but people seem to go out of their way to trivialize!

Whatever happened to the "Good 'ol days" when people went to church on Sunday and actually read scriptures and sang hymns and made some attempt to observe the Sabbath as a "day of rest"? Have we forgotten that God declared the Sabbath day to be sacred? Was he just kidding? Can God be pleased with the way people treat this special day?

Sports, politics and entertainment have pretty much taken over Sundays. God is all but forgotten, (except of course by the televangelists) and the search for personal gratification and fun has become the new religion of the day.

There's got to be a good reason God instructed us to reverence this day. I'm quite sure he didn't give us this commandment simply to round out his "Top Ten". So why do we trivialize it so much? Is this commandment really a big deal?

May I suggest some activities that would be appropriate to do on this day? How about visiting the sick, the widows, and the orphans? Try helping the homeless, doing service for others and strengthening your families. In order for us to truly understand its importance, its significance and the blessings that can be derived from its proper observance, we need to live it!

"If any man shall do my will, he will know of the doctrine" Christ said. If you want to understand the blessings and the rewards that accompany the proper observance of this sacred day, you must actually live the law!

I'll tell you some of the rewards you can expect to receive when you live this law. Your health will improve. Your body will actually get some well deserved rest, and be rejuvenated for the coming week's labors. Your family will grow stronger as you worship together. You'll take time to be with your children, to discuss important issues and grow in love and unity as a family. Your minds will be clearer as you give your mind a rest from its normal daily chores. It's also the perfect time to speak to your children about spiritual and moral choices; teaching them values that will make them better citizens and neighbors, and strengthening your home.

You'll be a better spouse as you take the time to unwind and eliminate some of the stresses which may have built up during the week. It's a great time for mom AND dad to help out with kitchen duties and visit friends and family. You'll be better parents as you spend some serious time with your children. Your understanding of life and love will increase as you study and ponder the scriptures, and many other blessings can and will come your way, as you keep the commandments of God.

Remember, it's for our good that God established this special day! He doesn't need the rest.

Number Five

Honor thy father and thy mother, that thy days may be long upon the land which the Lord thy God giveth thee.

This is the first commandment given with a promise; the promise of a long life.

Today, many children not only don't honor their parents, but they're taught in school, on TV and by their peers that parents often are nothing more than buffoons... goof-balls in adult bodies. Children are even taught that they're "individuals" as well, and should be able to be independent and make their own decisions without being influenced by "old fashioned thinking".

More often than not, these "enlightened" kids end up rebelling against their parents if their parents attempt to discipline them at all.

Often, in defiance, they turn to drugs, sex and alcohol. (Sometimes kids turn to these things **with** the encouragement of parents! Those kinds of parents really ARE screwed up!)

Assuming parents DID teach their children proper Christian values, and our children lived those values, think how many young lives could be saved from death, immorality and social ruin. When you consider how many thousands of kids and adults die each year as a result of drunk driving, drugs and drug deals gone bad, sexually transmitted diseases, AIDS and suicide, it's simply heartbreaking.

If parents would take the time to teach correct values, and if children would listen to and be obedient to their parents, many of our nation's ills would disappear practically overnight.

Life can and should be long and happy, but when there are no guidelines or limits set, no discipline or self-control encouraged or practiced, unhappiness will nearly always be the end result.

Number Six

Thou shall not kill.

This, perhaps more than any other commandment is relatively easy for the average Christian to live. After all, murdering another person, snuffing out another person's life for those with any conscience at all is absolutely unthinkable!

In no other area does the conscience of man shout louder that a particular act is wrong, than it does when it involves the taking of a human life. And thank heaven for that!

But some individuals are so rigid when it comes to defining "killing", that for many of us we don't even consider the possibility that God is speaking of much more than simply one grown person taking the life of another grown person.

What of those who are the most helpless, the most innocent of all human beings? What of the children "yet unborn"?

This is an issue that's caused more contention, evoked more emotion, and angered more people than almost any other issue in the history of our nation... and rightly so. I'm speaking of the practice of so-called "abortion".

Abortion is a horrible thing. But it goes so much deeper than simply a "decision" we might casually make. It's much more than just a "personal" choice. This decision has lasting, irreversible and often emotionally devastating consequences for everyone involved.

Let me interject a story here that I think demonstrates how far we've deteriorated morally in just my short lifetime.

When I was a young boy in the 1950's I lived in "the country" and had lots of farm animals. I think living on a farm actually gives young people a great advantage over city folk, simply by virtue of the fact that they're living with nature, and many of nature's lessons are learned "naturally".

On one occasion, I wanted more ducks for the farm, and rather than purchase mature ducks, I decided to take about twenty fertile duck eggs into a local hatchery and have them incubate the eggs for me.

I went to the hatchery, and the owner, a man I knew and respected, asked me if I'd like to go on a tour of the facility. I said sure!

As I toured the plant, however, I was shocked and actually *sickened* as I entered this one particular room. It was the room where the newly hatched baby chicks were "sexed", to determine whether or not they would be allowed to live.

You see, only the female chicks were kept alive, as they would be sold to egg farms as laying hens. Roosters were useless, and therefore were simply discarded.

I'd never given it any thought before that day. I suppose it made sense from a business standpoint, but my young impressionable mind wasn't prepared for what I was about to see.

As I watched the workers grab the chicks, several things struck me. First of all, they seemed very careless with these tiny creatures; even rough and heartless in my opinion.

The workers would take them in their hand, give them a quick squeeze and a flip to force out any poop that the chick might be about to drop, and in the same motion, they would check to see if the chick was male or female. If female, they were returned to a box with hundreds of other female chicks. If however they were male, they were simply thrown into 55 gallon drums, where they would run around frantically, trampling the chicks beneath them, struggling to stay on top of the dead or dying chicks, literally fighting for their lives.

When I saw this, I was absolutely sickened! I wanted to cry, but "big" boys weren't supposed to cry... that wouldn't have been cool, so I bit my lip and left the room. That horrible experience took some time to get out of my young impressionable mind.

It would be many years before I had a similar but much more disturbing experience... this time, however, it wasn't with baby chicks.

When I was about thirty years old, my wife and I were asked to take young women into our home who had "gotten in trouble". They would stay for six or eight months while their babies developed, during which time these young girls would make the difficult decision whether to keep the baby, or give it up for adoption.

As you can imagine, this was a traumatic experience for all these young girls. Often, these young women would receive information from different groups or individuals about options and programs available to assist them during this time of emotional turmoil.

On one occasion, one of the girls received in the mail some photos, taken by an attending nurse in an abortion clinic in Canada. This nurse had been involved with abortions for many years, but finally had to quit when her conscience got the best of her.

She sent pictures of fetuses and tiny babies, some of them still alive, who'd been thrown into a large drum, bloody and helpless, waiting to die and be discarded. What she *claimed* had caused her to finally quit was a particular experience she'd had with a little baby that was aborted nearly full term, and then left in the garbage to die. She removed it from the garbage and took it to a broom closet, where she sat for hours, holding it and meditating about what she was participating in . This baby absolutely would have lived, but Doctors refused to allow that to happen.

When I saw those photos, (taken long before Photo Shop was invented) I was sickened beyond belief. I couldn't imagine any humans being that calloused or evil. I knew Hitler and Stalin and other evil men had engaged in similar kinds of hellish behavior, but I never imagined that people in a free "Christian" society would ever allow such atrocities to occur!

I believe there are rare circumstances such as incest, rape or the ACTUAL concern for the life (not lifestyle) of the mother, which do and should play a role in this very contentious debate. However, such abortions should be performed within the first few weeks after conception! Certainly NOT after the baby has developed completely to become a beautiful little human being. The ugly truth is that 99.9% of the 1.3 million abortions performed in this country annually are the result of stupidity, immorality, lack of self control, selfishness and blatant disregard for the commandments of God.

The most glaring, despicable form of abortion is the so-called "partial birth" procedure. This practice could and should be more aptly described as "Pre-delivery murder"!

(I'd written six paragraphs giving a description and my opinion of this hellish procedure, but it made me feel so ugly inside to even read over it again that I deleted it in order to protect those with delicate feelings. All you need know is that this kind of evil is what makes that bumper sticker I read on back of the car in Chico California so true.)

Now there may be some who are skeptical of the story I've shared above. For those who are, note that it's a matter of record and easily verified, that then State Senator Barak Obama helped push through and passed a bill into law in Illinois, stating that **any baby born alive during an abortion procedure, must be left to die... and could NOT be assisted or rescued by any person.** This kind of evil is far too common in our "Christian nation". This is NOT the kind of act that endears us to a loving God.

Does anyone seriously believe that killing innocent babies in this manner will go un-noticed by God? I'd hate to be in these doctors shoes when they're brought to stand before God and try to explain why they shouldn't be room-mates with Hitler.

Number Seven

Thou shall not commit adultery.

This is one of the most important commandments of all, and one which has the most far reaching personal, family and social consequences, yet it's routinely ignored. In fact, this sin, more than almost any other serious sin is actually *embraced* by the people in Hollywood!

To understand just how perverted society has become, and how ridiculous the liberal media is, look at what we are willing to accept in America today. One well known U.S. Senator received "Father of the Year" award six months AFTER he confessed to having an affair with another woman! Really? Father of the Year? Since when did infidelity and immorality become unimportant and trivial, even a "non-issue" as it relates to being a good parent?

Some rationalize that because "adultery" is defined as sexual relations between *married* people who have taken "sacred vows" together, that sex *before* marriage (fornication) isn't really that big a deal... after all, "everyone's doing it!" This of course is the rationalization they hope everyone will embrace and accept to ease their conscience. But God does NOT accept that as an excuse.

Fornication is the ugly stepsister to adultery, and either sin, if not repented of, will keep us from entering the kingdom of God.

When the rich young man questioned Christ and asked him what he had to do to inherit eternal life, Christ told him that he needed to keep *ALL the commandments!* If conformity and obedience to all the commandments were the requirements for that young man then, we can with certainty conclude that keeping ALL the commandments of God is also pre-requisite for us too if we wish to enter into His Kingdom. (And yes, the commandments he spoke of include the Ten Commandments... all of them!)

The sanctity of the family is of paramount importance to God, and adultery and fornication do more to destroy the family unit than almost any other sin mentioned in holy writ.

Marriage is ordained of God, and has been correctly defined as the sacred union between one man and one woman.

There are obvious reasons for this of course, namely that married people are commanded by God to multiply and replenish the Earth. And two loving parents, one male, and one female, is the ONLY combination that makes pro-creation possible and acceptable in the eyes of God. And one male and one female is ALWAYS "naturally" the best combination for raising spiritually, socially and emotionally balanced children.

Sexual activity within marriage is the *only* process designed and approved by God for populating the earth with bodies that will house the spirits of His children. Wholesome sexual relationships *within* the bonds of marriage strengthen marriage and the family.

This is the one act where man and woman work in direct partnership with God to bring about the renewal of life and the perpetuation of mankind here on earth.

The miracle we call birth is the one and only area where God has entrusted to human beings the sacred opportunity of creating life, acting in partnership with Him to bring children into this world.

It takes both sexes to accomplish this work, and God has declared the union of marriage as the only legitimate partnership to accomplish it.

The sexual drive in man was placed there by God to guarantee the survival of the species; however, He also established guidelines and laws that if followed, will result in happiness and prosperity. If ignored and mocked, however, it will result in misery and regret, whether in this life or the next.

It doesn't take a genius to recognize that in nature, the animals of the world are driven mainly by instinct. The most powerful drive in most of the animal kingdom is the drive to reproduce, to mate with the strongest and the best specimens available to guarantee the survival of the fittest.

As we look at society today, one has to wonder if mankind has sunk to a lower level than even the animals. Many people, perhaps a majority of the world, have sunken to a lower level than even the animals, because they primarily desire sex not for the good or the survival of the human race, but simply to fulfill their own perverted sexual urges.

It used to be that people would date for a while in order to get to know the person they felt some attraction towards. Relationships were built on trust, common interests, common goals, and thoughtful planning of future expectations and family ambitions.

Today, however, we have degenerated and fallen to basically the same or a lower level of existence than the animals. With most people, young or old, the first thing on their mind is "how does this person perform sexually", and they usually discover the answer on their first date! God is displeased and angered with this shallow and degrading shift in principle and social practice.

When I was a young man preparing to go out on my first date with a girl, my father had a talk with me about the "fairer sex". He sat me down and communicated clearly his expectations as it related to my **responsibilities** as a man. He said that these rules of courtship were the accepted rules and standards of society and I was expected to live them. These are the instructions he gave to me...

"Son... when you take out a young lady on a date, you take upon yourself some serious responsibilities. First and foremost, you are responsible for the safety and protection of that young lady...no matter who she is.

"You make sure that you treat her with respect... and you protect her from every kind of danger. Remember that she is first and foremost a daughter of God, and therefore must be treated like a princes!

"You treat her with kindness and respect, and never do anything that would be hurtful, embarrassing or offensive to her or her parents... or you'll answer to me first, and then you'll have to answer to God.

*"Don't you **ever** do anything immoral... and don't allow anyone else to hurt her or take advantage of her.*

"I expect you to defend her honor with your life! It's far better for you to die, defending her honor, than to live and bring dishonor to her or any other daughter of God!"

These were the instructions and the warnings my father gave to me. I had no question what his priorities were, and what he expected from all his sons.

I suppose that here is the appropriate place to mention other types of sexual sin.

One of the huge priorities of the liberal socialists' agenda today is to push the goals of the so-called "gay" community. This is disturbing, unhealthy, offensive to God and profoundly wrong.

Many argue that this isn't sin at all... after all, they often protest... "I was born this way."

Now this is going to come as a shock to many of you, but I believe these individuals probably were born "that way". But here's what we all need to understand in order to have an intelligent discussion as to whether or not that makes it right or acceptable.

First of all, every individual born into this world is born with specific "flaws" unique to themselves. It's a part of what makes each one of us interesting and special. Some have the natural urge to lie. Some are strongly compelled to steal or cheat, or take advantage of others. Some are predisposed to be bullies and take advantage of those who are weak, while others are born to crave sex. Every evil act has its roots and its beginnings in natural or fallen carnal man, *and all of us belong to that group of people.*

By the same token, every person also comes into this world with positive and uplifting gifts and personality traits... to help offset the negative ones. Fortunately, it's just the "evil" or "destructive" traits we need to work to eliminate in our lives as we work to strengthen and cultivate our positive virtues.

God knew of course that men were destined to be born in this fallen state, and that's precisely why he gave us parents to love, guide and direct us, the Bible to teach us, and a conscience to influence us; to assist us as we work to overcome the *natural evil tendencies* we all possess.

But the fact that we naturally want to lie, or steal, or cheat, or bully, or commit sexual transgression in any way, is not a legitimate reason to do any of those things. On the contrary, that's precisely why we need to develop the strength of character required to fight those tendencies. God has emphatically declared all these things to be wrong, and he's warned us that giving in to these desires will destroy us in the end.

Homosexuals argue that they're being singled out unfairly because of their "lifestyle choices". That's ridiculous! They're not being singled out any more than any other group who embrace wrong choices, but they have cleverly shifted the focus of the discussion to make it seem as though they have become "victims".

God's clearly pointed out and called to repentance all those who lie, cheat, steal, commit adultery, fornication, or any sexual act outside of marriage, as well as the hypocrites, the blasphemers, the disrespectful, the extortionists and on and on and society should reject *all* these sins because they are destructive to humanity and to society.

If you think about it, using their flawed logic, the next step is to establish special protections and advocacy groups to protect liars, thieves, adulterers, pedophiles, murderers and every other person involved in any of the activities forbidden by God.

The bottom line is simply this... those of us who suffer from the natural tendencies to "lust" after other women, to lie, to cheat, to steal, or do any other evil act, must learn to fight those feelings, repent when needed, and strive to become the kind of person Christ expects us to be. And he expects much from each of us. Jesus Christ himself gave us the charge to... **"Be ye therefore perfect, even as I, or your Father which is in Heaven is perfect."** I don't think he was just making idle chit chat. Christ said it, and that should be our ultimate goal if we *honestly* claim to be Christians.

And those who have homosexual tendencies are no different than all the other people who suffer with sinful desires. They need to repent, suppress their desires, and become more like Christ commands all of us to be. They're just like any other person who has personal struggles and shouldn't be given any special treatment or consideration. (They certainly won't be given a pass by God.)

Homosexuals are clearly no different than any other group of sinners... but for some reason they believe they ought to be treated differently. They're not "special", they're just more vocal, more organized, more obvious, more obnoxious, more belligerent and less repentant and rational. But God does not now nor has he ever condoned sexual sin regardless of what people say and despite the ridiculous laws corrupt governments may enact to accommodate them.

The Bible teaches us that God is "never changing"... so what in the world makes people think he'll make an exception when it comes to "gays"?

The question that arises then is this... should people hate and persecute homosexuals? The answer... of course not! That too would be contrary to God's teachings! Should we hate liars and thieves? No. Neither should we hate adulterers, fornicators or even murderers for that matter. In fact, Christ has commanded us to "love everyone... **even our enemies**", no matter what they may be guilty of. *Because if we choose to hate and persecute those who don't live as we believe they ought to live, then we too are guilty of serious sin which will keep us out of Heaven.*

Christ showed us the perfect example of how we ought to treat sinners. St. John chapter 8, verses 1-11 tells the following story:

When Christ was teaching in the Temple one day, a group of men brought a woman to him who was an adulteress. They had, as they said, "caught her in the very act".

They reminded him that the Law of Moses taught that such a person should be stoned... but they wanted to see if they could trip him up by getting him to say something contrary to accepted Jewish law and custom.

But Christ knew their thoughts. He read their minds and understood perfectly their motives. So, he simply knelt down, wrote something in the sand and without looking up said... *"Let he who is without sin, cast the first stone."*

Then something amazing happened.

These men were convicted of their unholy plot by their own seared consciences, and one by one they left, shamed and silenced.

When Jesus looked up, he asked the woman... *"Where are these thine accusers? Hath no man condemned thee?"*

"No man." Was her reply.

Then Jesus said unto her, *"Neither do I condemn thee: go, and sin no more."*

The way he treated this woman was compassionate and instructive! He didn't say "Keep up the good work". He didn't say, "Adultery isn't really *that* bad of a sin." He certainly didn't say... "Do whatever you like, as long as it makes you feel good". He didn't say... "That's ok... you were probably just *born* that way." He didn't excuse her actions in any way!

What he DID say was this... "Neither do I **condemn** thee... go thy way and *sin no more*." Here was the one and ONLY person qualified to judge, condemn and punish this woman, and he did none of those things. Instead, he set the example for each of us. He acknowledged that her actions were sinful, and lovingly encouraged her to turn from sin and start back on the path of righteousness.

That should be our message as Disciples of Christ. We cannot do more; He would not expect us to do less.

The thing that makes so many people angry with the "gay" community is simply this... they flaunt their actions publicly and **literally** parade themselves through town, knowing that many people of all religious persuasions are deeply offended by their actions. And it's offensive because *this lifestyle has been forbidden by God*... yet they don't seem to care at all for the feelings or beliefs of anyone but themselves. They have this arrogant "in-your-face" attitude that doesn't endear them to mainstream Christianity. In fact, they treat everyone else exactly the same way they say they hate to be treated. It's a vicious evil cycle.

How would they feel if thieves, liars, bullies and murderers flaunted their sins publicly and mocked their deeply held personal beliefs? How *do* they feel when hateful individuals mock them and say hurtful things? It's interesting that they're the only group of transgressors who actively mock Christ's teachings and don't care who they offend. But offending God publicly and mocking those who do choose to obey His word will come back to haunt them in the end.

Remember, although we as individuals may strongly disapprove of the way some people choose to live their lives, the one thing that true Christians must always fight for is the right to make our own choices. That is also a tenant of Christianity. And those who would take that right away from others, are the most evil of all people.

Number Eight

Thou Shall Not Steal.

Here's a fact of life... when times get tough, the true character of individuals or nations is often revealed. So, let's take a moment and look at some of the calamities that have struck this world in recent years, and see how different cultures have reacted.

When Katrina struck New Orleans, one of the major stories that emerged over time was the wide-spread looting that took place. Some argue that people were simply trying to survive, but many first hand accounts reveal that in its aftermath, people were breaking into many places of business... places that didn't sell food or other "survival" items, and were simply taking whatever they wanted. One man was heard saying that the store he was taking from was "every mans store now", and showed no remorse as he walked away with many items of expensive clothing. Many people were stealing TV's and electronics, and the New Orleans police department reported they had been given permission to "shoot looters".

When young hoodlums in London decided to go on a destruction rampage, hundreds of these punks began burning businesses down, looting and stealing items just for the fun of it. This scenario has been repeated in many countries.

Now compare those actions with what happened in Japan after the March 2011 earthquake and tsunami.

ABC News reported that after the quake, thousands of wallets washed up on the beaches of Japan or were otherwise found in the rubble, containing a total of $48 million dollars in cash... and all of it was given willingly to authorities so they could locate the rightful owners! Also, 5,700 safes containing over $30 million in cash have been returned to the authorities who have worked tirelessly to restore that money to its rightful owners.

When you watched the news coverage of Katrina, there were fights, chaos and anger everywhere. Contrast that with the dignity of character displayed by the Japanese people. Even those who were extremely hungry and had to wait in lines to receive food did so with order, calm, respect and class. What was the difference?

I think the major reason these reactions were so opposite is because the Japanese people have religious and social values that loving parents engrained deeply into the hearts and minds of their children. America on the other hand, has in large measure lost its moral compass because it's incrementally pushed aside religious values and teachings, replacing them with the selfish desires of the "natural man." Americans in large part have become selfish, putting their personal desires above that of family or society.

In Japan, honor is paramount, and as a nation, we would do well to learn from their example. For all the great advances that America's given to the world, this is one area where we are falling behind. It seems like the general dishonesty in America today is just considered to be "the way it is."

Has America lost its sense of honor? Do we really NOT understand the principle of HONESTY? Have we simply resigned ourselves to the "fact" that no one is totally honest anymore, so let's just not worry about it?

My mother would have forced me to walk five miles through snow to return a nickel or a stick of gum if I'd stolen it from someone. And she'd be right behind me every step of the way with a switch in hand, whacking me if I didn't move as fast as she thought I should. With my parents, character DID matter! But I fear that America has lost its collective conscience. I hope I'm wrong; if not, we're in for some rocky times ahead.

And the fact that politicians, movie stars, celebrities, and many other prominent people set shameful examples in these as well as many other areas of life doesn't mean that we shouldn't be outraged by their behavior.

We should all be upset at the lack of honesty and morality in America, and we shouldn't brand those who make an attempt to be honest as "prudes" or "holier-than-thous"!

Again, God gave us this commandment for a good reason, and for nations to survive and society to excel, they must have order, honesty and the rule of law. When nations become so corrupt that they ignore these basic commandments, total destruction isn't far off. Dishonesty is also a sin, and any sin not repented of, will keep us out of Heaven.

Number Nine

Thou Shall Not Bear False Witness Against thy Neighbor.

For those who may not understand "Bible Speak", this simply means don't lie! And it's not just about lying to your neighbor, your Pastor or your spouse.

A man's word, his honor, is looked upon today as something that may be nice to have, but not nearly as important as a legally binding document. Some look at honesty as an old-fashioned value that's "nice" but it isn't really that important anymore. People have come to believe that "little white lies" are not only acceptable but even quite humorous at times... some would argue that they're even "charming".

Politicians are especially skilled in the art of pseudo-outrage as they sanctimoniously condemn political opponents when they believe they can raise the ire of the citizenry and further their own agenda by doing so. They think nothing of casting their opponents in a bad light when it furthers their agenda, yet it's only "partisan bickering", and part of some "vast right wing conspiracy" when it isn't in **their** best interest.

And the liberal media lovingly embrace's this perverted agenda of deception and lies. Shame on the politicians and the media who maliciously manipulate stories and pervert "facts" for personal or political gain!

One of the most glaring but apparently successful advertising campaigns on television in recent times is one that absolutely mocks all the most basic and godly virtues espoused by Christianity.

The disgusting ad campaign I'm speaking of is the one that states that "What happens in Vegas stays in Vegas!" Really?

Some perverted advertising executives obviously believed this was a clever idea, and so too must the people of Nevada who pay for it. I'm not sure who's responsible for this ad campaign, whether it's the Las Vegas Gaming Commission, the City, or the State of Nevada itself, but whoever it is, I have just one thing to say to you. Shame on you! Are you really that corrupt, that decadent and irresponsible? Do you actually condone this type of behavior? Are you really that stupid, that shallow, and that immoral?

I suppose these ads are clever... to morons and infidels; but they are nothing but disgusting and offensive to anyone with any degree of intelligence and morality.

What's the message they're trying to get out? It's simply this... "Anything immoral is welcome in Vegas! - And we won't tell your wife, your girlfriend, your husband, your boyfriend, your minister... Nobody has to know! So come to Vegas, betray the trust of everyone who cares about you! Thumb your nose at God and his commandments; hey, it's all in GOOD FUN! And remember... "What happens in Vegas stays in Vegas!"

Only that's the big lie, isn't it? STD's have this horrible habit of following people home! Dishonesty reveals itself at the most inopportune times! (We see this with congressman, sports professionals and others who don't take seriously their wedding vows.) And personal betrayal has a way of rotting relationships, destroying love and eroding trust over time, always ending in heartache, misery, and shattered lives.

What happens in Vegas stays in Vegas? I don't think so!

Those shallow thinking individuals who make and pay for this ad campaign need to understand that what happens in Vegas, will probably destroy lives, families and the trust of innocent loved ones, and there's NO WAY the consequences of a persons evil actions will ever just "stay in Vegas"!

We need to be clear and honest here. What happens in Vegas will follow you to the grave and beyond! It will hurt your family and your loved ones. You *will* eventually be exposed and then everyone will realize that this ridiculous ad campaign wasn't really that funny after all!

Those who claim to be Christian cannot continue to thumb their noses at Christ without incurring serious, even catastrophic personal, family and social repercussions! God will not allow evil acts to go unpunished forever!

Number Ten

Thou Shalt Not Covet.

Do people even know what that word means anymore? If you don't, let me help you understand.

To covet means to "have an inordinate desire for that which belongs to another." In other words, you want something so much, that you loose perspective of the things that matter most in life.

In this country there's an epidemic of people who suffer from this fundamental character flaw.

Every day, children attack other children to steal I-Pods from them as they walk down the street listening to music. They beat up, and often even murder children who happen to be wearing expensive athletic shoes, simply because they "want them"!

These "children" obviously haven't been taught principles like honesty, hard work and other critical social and religious values in their homes. Most likely because their parents (or parent) were derelict in their obligations to teach them correct Christian values.

More often than not, these children come from broken or dysfunctional families themselves. Too often they come from single mothers, who got pregnant by some person who demonstrated no morals or self control, and had no intention of being a responsible father. His only interest was "sex and excitement"! Weak minded girls with low self-esteem fall easy prey to such predators.

It's an all too common story. The guy gets the girl pregnant, then simply walks away to let society deal with his immoral choices.

Hollywood and the music industry share much of the blame when it comes to corrupting these young foolish minds.

Look at what Hollywood and the music industry do in an effort to amass their "filthy lucre".

The movie industry spends millions showing the excitement and the "passion" of sexual permissiveness, deliberately destroying or at least corrupting the concept of the wholesome American family. They go out of their way to make fun of the "traditional" home, and are absolutely obsessed with making so called "sit-coms" with obvious non-traditional families and homosexual overtones.

Musicians rap and yell and make "music" that seems to hypnotize these brain numb children who get sucked in by the message and the beat, while young girls, scantily clad in the most provocative attire, gyrate and move in the most seductive ways imaginable, sending an unmistakable message that debauchery and permissiveness are cool and in style.

The sad truth is that many of our young people who view this stuff actually believe this is what life is all about, and they begin to emulate these "artists". Before you know it they're getting involved in drugs and gangs and every kind of sexual perversion as well. Is this really the America we want for ourselves and our children?

And then the thing these "entertainers" try to do to convince people that they really are responsible people and really do care about society is to make *Public Service Announcements* to air on TV telling kids to stay in school, don't have sex, don't do drugs, and don't join gangs. You know... all the things they just did on the video. Can anyone say hypocrisy?

Is it any wonder that thousands of our young children get into trouble every single day? But I digress... back to coveting.

It's not just kids or youngsters who have a problem with this concept. Many adults... even wealthy successful adults struggle with this evil.

They have plenty, yet it's never enough. They aren't content to simply keep up with the Jones's. They need to "out-do" the Jones's so there's no question in anyone's mind "who's really the best" or the "most successful".

Remember the "rich young man" we spoke of earlier?

After Christ told him he needed to keep all the commandments if he wanted to inherit eternal life, the young man replied...

"All these things I've kept from my youth up."

Now when Jesus heard these things, he said unto him, "Yet lackest thou one thing: sell all that thou hast, and distribute unto the poor, and thou shalt have treasure in heaven: and come, follow me."

And when he heard this, he was very sorrowful: for he was very rich.

And when Jesus saw that he was very sorrowful, he said, "How hardly shall they that have riches enter into the kingdom of God!

For it is easier for a camel to go through a needle's eye, than for a rich man to enter into the kingdom of God."

(St. Luke 18: 21-25)

Having "enough" should make all of us grateful, yet all too often, "enough" just isn't good enough, because our pride demands that we appear "better" than the next guy.

Pride and covetousness are ugly flaws that will destroy each of us if were not careful.

CHAPTER EIGHT

AMERICAN NATION, CHRISTIAN FOUNDATION

This nation was founded by God-fearing men who were inspired by the Almighty to write our constitution. Intelligent thinkers have understood and accepted this fact from the beginning. But times are changing and history is being re-written.

There's a movement afoot by people who despise America's traditional values, to try to undermine or impugn the character of those early patriots in an effort to marginalize the work they accomplished. These are generally hateful people who despise God, and wish to advance their own secular agenda. These are people who consider themselves "progressive" in their philosophy, who look to Europe as the model of what they want this nation to become. And they want to "transform" America as quickly as possible. These individuals don't have a clue about who our founding fathers really were.

The founders of this great nation all had great faith in God, and believed that ALL men should have the freedom to choose how they would worship the God who created them. They didn't agree on all aspects of God or his character perhaps, but it was critical to them that they at least had the freedom to seek out and worship God in their own personal way.

Most of these men (or their ancestors) came from the British Isles where the Church of England *had* become the State Religion, having broken away from the Catholic Church on account of some "doctrinal disputes". (Thank you, Henry.)

These men recognized the evils inherent in a state run religion, and were determined that this nation would have a government that did nothing to coerce people into belonging to any particular religion, yet did everything to make it possible for individuals to pursue their own personal religious beliefs and goals. They knew that religion made people better... not worse citizens.

The law that protects this freedom is simple and beautiful, and is quoted here in its entirety. It's called the First Amendment.

Congress shall make no law respecting an establishment of religion, __or__ prohibiting the free exercise thereof; or abridging the freedom of speech, or of the press, or the right of the people peaceably to assemble, and to petition the Government for a redress of grievances.

This amendment is simple and straight-forward. It's so plain in its language that even a child should be able to understand it! (Perhaps that's why politicians and lawyers have struggled with it for so long.)

The huge danger here of course is that meddling and manipulating individuals, mostly perverted politicians, judges and lawyers, have attempted to corrupt the simple wording of this document to give new and very different meaning to its words.

They argue that anything religious in nature has no right to be displayed on public property. This perversion of the document is obvious to anyone with even ordinary intelligence.

Allowing religious expression on state or federal land is NOT establishing a state religion any more than cops carrying guns means that ALL of us are somehow being forced to start packing heat.

The fact that a Judge wears a black robe doesn't mean that we as citizens are obligated to become Goths.

Selling steaks does NOT mean that people aren't free to be vegetarians if they want to be!

Our founding fathers had no problem publicly proclaiming their "personal" belief in God, and allowing other people to do the same, because they knew that the first amendment was not written to make belief in God "less accessible", but "more accessible" to all who desired it!

Today however, the Anti-Christ-Litigation-Union (ACLU for short) has not only done everything in their power to pervert and corrupt the correct interpretation of this simple document, but they have invested millions of dollars into actively working to destroy Christianity in America. This, I believe, is their primary agenda.

They of course will deny it, stating that their primary concern is only for "us", the American people, and for the preservation of our "civil liberties". Whatever!

They're simply money grubbing socialist lawyers who will do anything and everything in their power to destroy America's belief in God while promoting their own secular agendas. And they've become so good at it, that generally by the time they finish their arguments, the simpletons they've "championed for" have no idea what they've really given up, and actually believe they've done a great service to society.

It's disgusting and troubling how these people will fight tooth and nail to preserve the "rights" of pedophiles, members of NAMBLA, perverts who encourage buggery of every sort, sex-fiends, child molesters, promoters of every sordid sexual act and people with blatant immoral agendas, yet when it comes to the issue of "God"... at least the "Christian God", they attack their beliefs like a rabid pit-bull.

Oh sure, they explain very passionately and convincingly that they're really only looking out for *everyone's* rights... our "civil liberties" and what's best for our nation, but don't believe that for one moment. These people are only interested in one thing... the ultimate overthrow and demise of this country as a "Christian" nation.

I'm certain there are some "dupes" working for them who have ignorantly been brainwashed into believing that they really are doing something very important and noble for this country, but those who may fall into that category are certainly the exception.

The ACLU, the "it's cool to be gay" groups, the amoral Hollywood Libs, the "Blame America First" crowd, the secular progressives, the "main-stream press" as well as ALL the other people who want Christ out of America and his teachings banned... these are the people who are the real threat to America.

These are the people we should be standing up against every single day! These are the people who seek to control all Americans, our thoughts and our actions. And they want to punish or destroy any and all who don't go along with their agendas.

The Islamo-terrorists aren't the real threat to this nation; they're just a distraction to divert our attention away from the more serious cancer that's already festering within our boarders and threatening the spiritual soul of America.

The biggest threats America face today aren't radical Muslims, the North Koreans, the Chi-Coms, Mexican immigrants, or even Iran and that mental midget Amidinajad; no, the real threat to America today are those evil or otherwise misguided individuals already residing within the borders of our country. It's the secular socialists who hide behind the skirts of Lady Liberty, demanding protection from those who would expose them, while actively working to destroy the very nation that's given them a home, protected them from would-be invaders and provided them with the educational and intellectual tools they now actively use against her! It's time we wake up and speak out to take America back! It's time we recognize the perilous path we're blindly being led down.

Man by his very nature is destined to become evil and corrupt UNLESS he YIELDS his will to Gods, and embraces the higher, more lofty principles God's revealed to us.

This "Christian" nation is being trampled on and systematically torn apart by people who are wolves in sheep's clothing, yet many of us are too blind to recognize them or understand their agenda.

In the name of tolerance, we jump on board with every sick immoral special interest group that comes down the pike. Movie stars have not only totally accepted the homosexual movement and their message, but they actively promote them so they don't incur their wrath or become ostracized by the Hollywood elite.

The art world has largely been hijacked by this same group as well as other sexual perverts, and anyone who disagrees with their views are brutally and viciously attacked, labeled as intolerant homophobes and their gifts and talents maligned or dismissed.

And how is it possible that so many people, corporations, news agencies and television stations have all jumped on the amoral anti-religion band-wagon, defiantly thumbing their collective noses at Christianity and the teachings of Jesus Christ, while this sleeping giant, supposedly 80% of all Americans who CLAIM to be Christians, sit idly by and refuse to take a stand concerning issues that God's been very clear on?

How on earth did we ever allow this very small minority to reshape the face of this once moral country? When will we find the courage to stand up and say "enough is enough"?

I for one do not want to see this nation go the way of Babylon, Greece, Rome, Hitler's Germany, France or any other nation that's fallen from grace.

I could care less what liberal nations like France, the Netherlands, the Scandinavian countries or even Canada think of us! It doesn't matter what any of them think! Who cares if they call us "prudes" for not sharing the same "values" they do? If we're truly "Christian", then isn't God's opinion the ONLY opinion that should really matter to any of us? If every nation on earth turned against us, we would still know that we were in the majority because as Christians we understand that... ***"If God be for us, who can be against us?"*** (Romans 8:31)

It's the moral corruption from within our own borders that will ultimately destroy us as a nation **unless** we change our thinking and change it fast! And if we eventually do fall from God's grace and are overrun by some invading nation, it will only be because WE have forfeited the right to ask for and merit God's protection. If we continue on the present course we're on, we shouldn't be surprised when God allows some foreign nation to not only invade our country and destroy us, but in fact, he may actually support and strengthen those invading armies as he allows *them* to exact *His* judgment and "cleanse the inner vessel" of the country that was once his most favored nation. If you think that cannot happen... I refer you to history. Every single nation in recorded history has fallen not long after they became sufficiently corrupt... and we will not escape justice either.

It's time to take back this country from those who don't support and sustain our constitution.

The godless will tell you that freedom from God is progress. But that's a lie. Freedom from God is bondage; bondage to Satan, to sin and to corruption. Without God, this nation has no future! Without God, there never can be true freedom.

Political correctness is the mental illness of modern society. We've been brainwashed into believing there's no such thing as good or evil; that everything's simply "preference".

By "softening the rhetoric", we're told that this nation will become a "kinder, gentler place". Another clever lie. The truth is, we'll simply become more corrupt, more decadent and in the end... "Godless". The United States at that point will have become just another unremarkable nation.

We're being told by liberal secularists that anyone who takes a stand on issues of morality, *as defined in the Bible*, are "hateful, judgmental and divisive"... many even go so far as to characterize Christ's teachings as "hate speech". Clever rhetoric by none other than Satan himself. It's literal fulfillment of prophecy in the Bible which states that in the last days, men would become so corrupt, they would actually call good evil, and evil good. *We have now officially arrived at that place.* We need to get back to the basic building blocks of Christianity, we need to once again shore up the foundation of morality that Christ taught in the New Testament.

Since when has perception become more important than reality? And is the truth only valid or permissible when it doesn't offend someone?

Don't get me wrong. We ought to be charitable; we ought to be forgiving when mistakes are made. But blatant intentional hypocrisy, deception and dishonesty change the game. Liars and hypocrites don't get a pass in my book! And as humans, we have to be honest at some point to protect ourselves, our families, our religion and society.

In America today, the prevailing thought is that you can say anything you like, be as rude and vulgar as you want, because it only makes you more interesting IF you're on the left or IF you're a so called "comedian".

But if you're on the right, or a "Christian" then you're a "_____ phobe", (you can fill in the blank) or you're a bigot, or judgmental or an evil Christian fundamentalist fanatic! And remember, according to some celebrities, fundamental Christians are as bad as Islamo-terrorists! And the press just gobbles up this garbage.

It's time to wake up America. It's time we begin to recognize these people for who they are and point them out when they try to subvert our freedoms, destroy our faith and ridicule our Savior. We **must** be able to discern good from evil, and we need to expose evil people for who they are in order to protect our children and our faith! And we must never allow others to believe that we accept or condone evil or deviant behavior simply because the media embraces it!

I'm saying that as a society, as a CHRISTIAN society, we need to pull our heads out of the sand and realize what's at stake here!

We all need to personally take a stand, and let the world know whose side we're really on!

We need to call a spade a spade, we need to recognize evil for what it is, and we need to have the courage to let our voices be heard!

I like our current Pope, Pope Benedict XVI, who has courageously taken a stand on many "*sensitive and divisive*" issues. He calls abortion evil, and homosexuality a sin. He states emphatically that Hell "is a *real* place" and says that evil people, people who fight against God and defy his commandments, will go to Hell!

Apparently the Pope doesn't care if that's offensive to some people! I say GOOD FOR HIM!

And we shouldn't care if it's offensive to people either! Remember, *a guilty conscience is what motivates people to have the desire to change their ways*. And correct me if I'm mistaken, but I don't recall ANY commandment that says... "Thou shalt not offend or make anyone feel uncomfortable in their sins."

I'm not at all concerned if Gods laws are offensive to murderers, fornicators, homosexuals, thieves, liars, adulterers, or the foul-mouthed individuals who constantly take God's holy name in vain. ***That's the whole reason God's given us a conscience!*** It's that uncomfortable feeling of being offended, or the fear that we're offending God, that motivates people to want to make changes in their lives! And remember... it's far better to offend people than it is to offend God!

The reason it's important that we as "Christians" try not to offend God is because when we leave this earth, all the money in the world won't be able to improve our situation there. (And make no mistake about it... ALL of us will eventually leave this life!) All the politicians in hell won't be able to pass a resolution to transfer you or I to a better facility or improve our surroundings. (And there'll be plenty of politicians there!) All the musicians, movie stars and lawyers who ever lived won't be able to force God to change his values or judgments or convince him to send sinners to a "kinder, gentler location". Celebrities and politicians may wield some influence in this P.C. world of corruption and decadence, but they have ***ZERO*** influence in Heaven! ***God is not infatuated with celebrities nor is he swayed by popular opinion or political correctness.***

Pricking the conscience of sinners, offending them, is precisely what God had in mind when he wrote the 10 Commandments! And he didn't intend for that reaction to change over the years. THAT'S WHY HE WROTE THEM IN STONE AND NOT IN SAND!

Being offended is precisely what motivates SANE people to see the error of their ways, to REPENT and make the changes necessary in their lives to merit Gods blessings! ***That has always been God's intent and the whole point of the Ten Commandments.***

CHAPTER NINE

THE "GLOBAL WARMING" FARCE

We're going to take a detour here and travel down a little side-street for a moment. (I just need a moment to "calm down".)

Intellectually honest scientists and historians concur that Earth's meager warming trend is neither unique, nor alarming. This earth, like every other living organism, is constantly changing in many ways, and surface temperature is merely one of those manifestations.

It's simply going through a natural cycle as it has thousands of times before.

For the earth to change 7/10ths of one degree in one hundred years, doesn't exactly qualify as a "global crises". These cyclical changes have gone both ways, cooler for a time then warmer for a time, for millions of years. That's no surprise, at least not to anyone with any degree of common sense and intelligence. But this current "crisis" is the most wonderful gift nature could possibly have come up with for liberals and the "godless intellectual elite" in America. This throws these people into a state of absolute mental and emotional euphoria. (This so called crisis isn't working out too well though, since global temperatures have actually been on the decline for most of the last decade. Hence, you don't hear much about "global warming" anymore. Nope, now it's global "climate change" which is so much more sophisticated and infinitely more defensible.)

Why, you might ask, would this make anyone happy? Let me offer some suggestions.

I believe liberals love "climate change" because this "crisis" is the perfect example in their minds to demonstrate the "wisdom and intelligence of man", while effectively (in their minds) debunking the foolish notion of an all powerful, all loving God.

This crisis is great because "logically", if their really WAS a God, he surely wouldn't allow this type of thing to happen. He'd just "reset the thermostat!" Either that or he's a callous, mean spirited God, so why would anyone want to worship him anyway?

Christians on the other hand, look back on history when there were catastrophes or plagues, and often view those events as warnings from God. God often used these type of events to get our attention and refocus our thoughts on things that have eternal consequences. "Natural calamities" have always been employed by God as "wake-up calls" for his children.

Catastrophes and natural disasters are not new, and certainly not unique to our day. History is littered with them. The only thing that's new about the "climate crisis" of today is the fact that man has actually become so arrogant, he seriously believes he can actually control the earth's temperature. I take that back... "serious scientists and thinkers" know they can't possibly make any real change... but serious "money-grubbers" realize this is a cash cow of "Biblical proportions". They know that if they can dupe the ignorant masses into believing this shtick, they can make more money with this scam than has ever been made in all of recorded history! And they're relying on the gullibility of you and me and the heavy-handedness of governments to accomplish just that!

Now the interesting thing about meteorological devastations of the past is that many of these "disasters" just happen to coincide with the moral corruption and decadence of the population at the time.

For example, look at the cities of Sodom and Gomorrah. God warned Lot and his family to flee the city because he said he was about to destroy them. His reasoning was, that the inhabitants of those cities had nearly all been sucked into embracing the sin we know as homosexuality, and God had finally had enough. This city was famous for its sexual perversions. It's where we got the word sodomy. (Sound familiar to anyone?)

So God destroyed these cities, which of course he had every right to do. In reality He simply took his children back to their former home to deal with them in his own way, removing them from this earth so they couldn't continue to corrupt his other children.

A very similar thing happened to another city in Italy named Pompeii. Pompeii had become the San Francisco of Italy, with all the same tourist traps and decadent immoral hot-spots.

The scientific community views it as a catastrophe that destroyed a "progressive" community. What really happened of course, is that God got tired of these people perverting themselves and polluting his other children, so he dumped Mt. Vesuvius on top of it.

The Roman Empire fell as a result of corruption from within. Sexual as well as political, spiritual and social deviants rotted that great empire. Their fetish with blood, gore, suffering and brutality all worked together to bring Gods judgments down on them. (Yes, God can even use barbarians to achieve his purposes.)

Virtually every major civilization on earth has fallen from power and been swept into the ash-heap of history as a result of moral corruption and decadence. From Caesar's Rome to Hitler's Germany, from Greece to Egypt, from the Incas and Aztecs to Spain, France and Britain, all have or will have to answer for their sins against God and humanity.

Each and every one of these nations enjoyed their "golden age" but now find themselves little more than a foot-note in history relegated to has-beens, or maybe legends and folk-lore.

The most disturbing realization, of course, is that the United States of America is without question, the most powerful nation on earth. But all that could change in the blink of an eye *if* God turns his back on us, or more accurately, *if we turn our backs on Him.*

And if the United States does collapse, it won't be because a bunch of turban headed terrorists infiltrated our borders and destroyed our nuclear facilities, or poisoned our drinking water, or sneaked in some deadly biological weapon. Nor will it be because of global warming and people using up too many of our natural resources.

Nope, if the U.S. collapses, it will be the result of moral decay from within, exactly the same way every other super-civilization on earth met its demise.

When God's finally had enough of the evil and corruption that's taken hold of this nation, he'll withdraw his blessing of protection and allow or possibly even support this nation's overthrow in order to cleanse the nation from the corruption of its people.

And people who think this is impossible are both arrogant and naive. Anyone who thinks my imagination is running away with my mind hasn't read the Bible and has no understanding of history or how God has dealt with his children throughout time.

The one sure fact of life is that history *always* repeats itself. That's what makes us humans look so incredibly stupid at times. We keep doing the same things over and over again; the same things that have always brought destruction and demise to civilizations of the past. In our feeble minds, we desperately hope that this time we'll experience a different outcome. (Isn't that the definition of insanity?)

America is teetering on the edge of destruction, and if we don't make some course corrections, some "Christian" adjustments, we're in for disasters that will make "global warming" seem like a visit to the tanning salon.

It's time this sleeping giant wakes up and takes control of our destiny from the godless socialists and liberals.

Make no mistake about it, global warming is a NON-ISSUE! Don't be fooled by "Chicken Little" imposters.

And don't worry Al about things getting too hot here on Earth. Worry instead about the temperature of the place we'll all go *after* this life! That's the only future you or I have any real control over; *and each of us can assure our future by choosing to follow God and keep his commandments starting today!*

CHAPTER TEN

THE PORNIFICATION OF AMERICA

The REAL GLOBAL WARMING issue we should all be worried about.

In Revelations, chapters 8 and 9, we read about the last days and the terror which is going to be unleashed upon this earth as a result of the evil and debauchery of its inhabitants.

We're told that one third of the earth's trees, the sea's creatures, animal life and even mankind itself will be destroyed as punishment for the wickedness of man. Most of this destruction will come as a result of fire and the accompanying devastation from weapons of war. *Now we're talking global warming!*

Yes Al, this earth *is* going to get hot, and lots of people are going to die. But it won't be as a result of automobile emissions, greenhouse effects, cows farting in the fields or people using more than one square of toilet paper on their visits to the loo. It won't be because our tires weren't inflated properly, or because the evil

Americans used up all the oil and natural gas deposits trying to be comfortable and make life more convenient for ourselves and others.

It will come about as a result of the wickedness and corruption of humanity, and God will allow it to happen because his children have trashed his teachings, defied his commandments, defiled his church and turned their backs on the God who created them.

Revelations 9: 20-21 reads as follows...

"And the rest of the men which were not killed by these plagues yet repented not of the works of their hands, that they should not worship devils, and idols of gold, and silver and brass, and stone, and of wood: which neither can see, nor hear, nor walk:

"Neither repented they of their murders, nor of their sorceries, nor of their fornication, nor of their thefts."

These are some of the things that will ultimately bring about the destruction of mankind on earth. Did you catch it? Murders, sorceries, fornication and thefts!

Sadly, these are things that are happening on a daily basis all around us, and with the exception of murder, all these "evils" are simply brushed aside, even embraced as "normal acceptable behavior"!

Let me go back again to one of my earlier points - the corruption and politically correct perversion of the English language.

When I was a little boy, the worst thing you could call a girl was a "slut". Simply uttering the word made people cringe, and saying it in jest would have guaranteed a good mouth-washing with a bar of Ivory soap!

And the reason we didn't insult girls by using that "nasty" word was very simple. Slut in those days meant... *"A promiscuous woman. Not restricted to one sexual partner."* And it was clearly understood that that "partner" should be their spouse. The word "slut", *described an act* which is forbidden by God, and which society roundly rejected back then, because it was considered immoral and unacceptable in our Christian nation! The word was *intended* to be an insult!

We knew that of course, and that's precisely why "nice" people *never* used it. It described *whores* (who of course are just sluts who get paid for their sexual sins... which by the way was *another* nasty word we weren't allowed to use) and society didn't condone or approve of that kind of language; **not because of the way those words sounded,** *but because of the immoral and unacceptable behavior those words described.*

But the world we live in today has become totally perverted compared to just a few short years ago. Our society and our language have both become unprincipled! What's become of our nation and our language?

Words **are** important and should be respected, if for no other reason than the fact that they are tools... tools of expression, tools that have meaning and were designed to help us share thoughts clearly. Words are a way to describe reality, and a way to intelligently communicate with each other. But today, so many of our words have morphed and become either corrupt or sterile. How can we as a society effectively communicate when the very words we speak have become devoid of meaning?

When a man who operates on a persons heart walks into a room, it's not an insult to call him "Doctor". That word, in fact, describes what he is. If a man builds houses for a living, we call him a "carpenter". That describes what he does... and everyone seems to be ok with that. When a woman has a baby, we refer to her as a "mother", and that's generally a wonderful thing. And when a person is sexually promiscuous, (meaning they have no problem having sex outside the bonds of marriage) we may rightly call them a "slut"... because that is the actual definition of the word. The word is not what's insulting to God... it's the act that's offensive to God, and should be to all people of morals and principles.

The ridiculous thing that's occurred in our country recently however is that these "nasty words" are still looked upon as "unsuitable" to use when describing a sexually promiscuous person, yet the sinful *behavior* these words describe has become not only acceptable, but is now unashamedly embraced by society, thanks in large measure to the liberal crowd in Hollywood!

Think about it... fifty years ago, if a girl and a boy went on a date and fornicated, they felt dirty, sinful and embarrassed! (Which is the appropriate spiritual and emotional response ... after all, what they did is against God's law of chastity, and that's how a conscience is supposed to operate.) If a father ***found out*** that a boy was taking advantage of his daughter, he probably would have gotten out his gun and shot him. (Or at the very least he would convince the boy he was about to shoot him!)

But now days, it's generally expected that people who go out on a "date" will conclude the evening with a little booze and a little sex. If you don't, you're looked upon as "prudish" or old fashioned.

But the fact is that **God still considers serial fornicators to be sluts and whores,** and as the Bible says, they will be banned from entering Heaven unless they repent! How is it possible that we have strayed so far from this important principle? What on earth has happened to Christian America?

Intelligent, thoughtful and honest people are forced to conclude that America has largely become a nation of sluts. And if that sounds offensive to anyone, I'm sorry... but it is *an indisputable fact by it's very definition!*

I just happened to be flipping through the channels on the TV one day, and accidentally stumbled across some "reality show" where young people all lived together in a communal type setting, to see who made a good match. (I guess that was the idea behind it... I'm not sure.) Anyway, I remember a few short years ago when this kind of garbage first debuted on TV. Then, you were left to speculate whether or not these "kids" actually got together and fornicated or not. (Not that anyone really doubted it.) But on this particular show, they had cameras mounted in each bedroom, and they showed all these unmarried "couples" *sleeping in the same beds*, and "making out" under the sheets. I suppose the next step is to simply remove the sheets!

These "Reality Show" producers who think up this filth are nothing but evil minded perverts and God is surely angry with them. And those individuals who participate in this debauchery <u>will have to answer to God</u> for their part in the corruption of society and the destruction of Gods children. Are there no Christians left in Hollywood today?

And it's not just the entertainment industry that's become corrupt. On the news just recently, I watched a news anchor interview several "professional therapists and educators" who not only *condoned* the act of fornication, but stated that it was actually "healthy" allowing the couple to "test drive" their relationship to make sure it was a good fit before they made any long term commitments! ***Surely Moses must be rolling over in his grave!***

Look at the facts! By definition, most of our young people (and I'm sad to say, our older people as well) do NOT confine themselves to one sexual partner. And that "partner", according to God, is supposed to be their SPOUSE... NOT their SIGNIFICANT OTHER! (That's the most ridiculous moniker these politically correct people have ever come up with. Does "significant other" mean the person I most want to be with when I offend God, or does it mean the person with whom I'd most like to share my communicable diseases?)

If a person considers themselves to be Christian, how can they possibly rationalize fooling around with other people outside the marriage covenant? God clearly declared that sex is to be enjoyed ONLY within the institution of marriage! PERIOD! He couldn't have been more clear on the subject! ***Sex was intended for marriage and procreation, not dating and recreation!*** God didn't give us the Ten Commandments simply to have us cast them aside or be modified by evil people to suit their individual lifestyles!

For any nation to survive, requires that the foundation of morality remain intact. And this Christian nation was built on the idea that God-fearing people would live according to the laws and commandments of God. Only when we adhere to God's laws of chastity and morality can we as a society provide a suitable environment for family and community to exist and flourish. Without morality, we become barely more than animals.

And if this offends or embarrasses you because you're participating in any of these things yourself, that's actually a good thing... because it means that at least for now, your conscience is still functioning. And God is trying to touch your soul and help you change your life. It means he loves you, and wants you to make changes in your life that will bring you true and lasting happiness.

I know it's difficult to change sinful habits. I understand it's harder to swim upstream than it is to float downstream, but floating downstream is the thing garbage does ... and drifting with the current has never been a character builder. It's easy to float... it requires no effort, but it offers no rewards. Turning away from sin is NOT easy... it was never intended to be... but it is worth it! It's worth the peace of mind you get, knowing that you don't have to worry about getting some STD because you or your spouse engaged in "risky sex".

It's worth keeping yourself clean, to be confident that your children and your spouse don't have to deal with disease or other complications and consequences associated with immoral and risky behavior.

Thanks to the folks in Hollywood and the Music and Art world however, sex has all but lost the sacred connotation it was intended by God to have. Those relatively few TRUE Christians who actually believe God was serious when he set boundaries for proper sexual conduct are looked upon today as weirdoes, prudes and fanatics.

I remember when things were different. I remember when a great singer by the name of Nelson Eddie sang a song that supported the principle of morality. Two lines from the chorus of that song went like this...

"For the passions that thrill love and lift you high to Heaven, are the passions that kill love, and make you fall to Hell."

It was true then... it's true today!

Today however, we live in a society where every sit-com, every movie, every music video, every advertisement is marinated in the disgusting slime of sexual perversion.

Actors in Hollywood make PSA's telling our children to stay away from drugs, alcohol and risky sexual behavior, then immediately turn around and make films or music videos glorifying everything they just told the kids to stay away from. They justify their hypocrisy by claiming that it's "art"; but most of our young people can't see any difference between "art" and "reality"; and quite frankly, in most cases, neither can I. Where is the art in offending God and corrupting his children?

I'm certain that God will not accept the lame excuse artist's always fall back on when they attempt to rationalize their propagation of filth by claiming their craft is, and I quote... "a legitimate art form", and therefore shouldn't be criticized as immoral, but "should be viewed through the prism of entertainment and creativity!" Make no mistake... God *will* hold them responsible for the filth they produce, especially when it destroys the minds and the souls of our youth!

I'm proud to admit that I, for one, *do* believe that God was serious when he wrote the Ten Commandments in stone, (signifying that they would never become outdated) and I know for a fact, that "the Big Ten" are NOT that hard to live!

I understand first hand the peace of mind and happiness that came to me as a result of "saving" myself for my wife only. And I'm grateful she did the same for me.

I hope that doesn't sound boastful. But really, no one in this world should ever have to apologize or feel embarrassed for simply doing those things God's commanded *all* of us to do anyway! We should never be ashamed to admit that we actually DO try to obey God's commandments!

I'm getting very frustrated because it's just about impossible to turn on the TV anymore without seeing something on the television that's morally offensive, demonstrating this disgusting pre-occupation the world has with perversion, sex and the constant mockery of all things sacred.

I'm tired of the news people constantly showing the inappropriate sinful lifestyles of the Hollywood crowd on the morning and evening news, and then pretending they can't figure out why America is so fascinated with the private lives of these individuals. What hypocrisy! Most people would never even give these people a second glance, but the producers of the "news" have determined that everyone should be just as infatuated with this filth as they are, so they continue to serve it up on television because they believe it gets them higher ratings.

Do people not understand that if you constantly immerse yourself in sin and filth that it will eventually become a part of your character and personality? Satan certainly understands that principle!

You can't watch anything on television today without sex being dragged into it. It's like the people at the ad agencies have all lost their creative minds, and resigned themselves to the fact that they aren't smart enough to sell a product on its own merits, or by showing something clever or witty. So instead of using clever or clean humor, they just chuck it into the blender of sleazy sex and hope some dope will bite!

Is anyone else in America embarrassed or outraged as I am whenever another ad comes along on TV showing the latest in "feminine protection"? What ever happened to propriety? Am I the only man who gets irritated when "Bob" comes on the tube with that stupid grin on his face ostensibly because he's just taken some of his *male enhancement pills* and he's now exploding with testosterone and ready for some "action"?

How am I supposed to explain that kind of trash to my grandkids when they come to visit? (Who knows, maybe they've already learned all about that stuff in school or on the bus.)

Where is the outrage from the moral majority when we see "professional therapists" visit Boulder Colorado **High School** and *encourage* kids to "experiment with sex", (either male or female or any other combination they'd like), and, oh yes, "try out some drugs to enhance the experience while you're at it." (Do you remember that disturbing story?) However, the professional pervert in this story did try to come off as being a little responsible I suppose, suggesting that the younger children probably ought to start out with "simple masturbation." (I can only assume that's his version of sex on training wheels.)

WHAT ON EARTH ARE THESE SCHOOL ADMINISTRATORS THINKING WHEN THEY INVITE **EVIL** PEOPLE LIKE THIS INTO THEIR SCHOOLS? (YES... I SAID **EVIL** PEOPLE!) WHERE ARE THE GROWNUPS WHO ARE SUPPOSED TO BE RUNNING THESE INSTITUTIONS AND WATCHING OUR FOR OUR CHILDREN?

This kind of debauchery makes me very angry. (As you can tell... sorry about yelling.) But what kind of a future are we forging for our children?

This country is going downhill faster than a jack-rabbit on a date, and most people simply seem to be content to just sit back and watch it all happen.

As a nation we've become obsessed with this idea that we can somehow fend off old age and live out our lives just as handsome and horny as we were when we were twenty. Yep, that's what's really important in life... being able to find two bathtubs, side by side on some romantic beach, or high in the mountains somewhere hidden from public view (or not) where we can sit around and wait for "whenever the moment is right". And all this is made possible because we've spent our hard-earned money on that little blue pill, or one of a dozen other miracle pills that artificially jack up our libido to make us become the lovers we never were!

Is it any wonder we never hear about "great thinkers" any more? In years gone by, men grew old gracefully as "nature" quietly stepped in and subtly lessened the recurring urge men naturally had when they were younger, and replaced those desires instead with the "occasional" treat, leaving men time to contemplate the deeper meaning of life, study the great philosophers or ponder the wonders of the universe.

But not any more! Forget philosophy, forget pondering the universe, forget the search for wisdom, forget trying to teach the rising generation that the "golden years" are the ideal time for serious contemplation and personal introspection... I mean... who wants that when you've got that little blue pill?

What's happened to our society? Does any serious God-fearing Christian really believe this is how God intended for man to live out his days on Earth? Does anyone who honestly believes we're God's children, really think this full-time obsession with sex is remotely pleasing to our creator?

Sex, in and of itself of course, is not evil. But this constant flaunting of everything sexual is. It's shallow and it's degrading. It cheapens humanity, and it's absolutely disgusting to correct thinking, God-fearing people everywhere.

Don't delude yourself; God's not the least bit pleased with the perverted path America currently finds itself going down. This is the path to spiritual and social ruin, just as surely as it was for every other civilization that rose and fell throughout history.

We're witnessing for ourselves an all-out assault on modesty, morality, the traditional "family" and the principles and traditions that Christians have long considered sacred. Major media networks are doing everything in their power to push their amoral agendas, promote nudity and homosexuality by constantly pushing the envelope of decency and legality.

Even the word FAMILY has been hijacked and corrupted by the libs and anti-Christ factions in our country.

Family used to mean "parents and their children". Extended family meant the blood relatives of those individuals.

Today, however, family can mean anything you want it to mean. Six friends living together, jumping each other whenever they feel like it... abra-ka-dabra... a family. Two homosexuals living together and pretending to be just like a real couple... poof... it's a "family". They even try to add credibility to themselves and their "family" by getting a child to take care of one way or another. Some choose to adopt a baby so they can feel "just like real parents do". The problem with that, of course, is that you actually end up messing up an innocent child who is now being raised by a couple of individuals who have consciously chosen to mock the teachings of God by thumbing their noses at conservative Christianity. And as a result this poor little child has virtually no chance of ever having the positive opportunity to experience the happiness they could have experienced if they'd been adopted into a *true traditional* family.

They're basically doomed to live life morally, socially, and spiritually handicapped; the same as if they'd been adopted by parents who openly embrace any of the other sinful character flaws *common to man **yet forbidden** by God.*

I understand that when some people read this, they're going to be absolutely appalled to think that anyone could be so "judgmental", so "bigoted", or such a "hate-monger"! Believe me... I'm none of those things and I never have been. I love everyone... but that's *not* the issue here and you know it.

Please remember this... I didn't make up the rules or the definitions of correct moral and social behavior and neither did you... God did! And He's the ONLY individual qualified to do so! And it's all explained right there in the Bible! It's been the gold standard of morality for thousands of years, and has been shown time and time again to be the **only** recipe for success and lasting happiness in society. And if you don't like the things I'm saying, you can throw away the Bible, you can denounce religion and even deny the reality of God, but do NOT say that I am the author or originator of any of these concepts. *If you don't like the message, don't kill the messenger!* Take it up with the one who set the standards. Take it up with the one who will assign us our eventual rewards after this life. Take it up with the one who gave us the ten commandments, died for us on the cross and authored the message of salvation, hope and love... and in this case, that would be GOD!

I could obviously go on for hundreds of pages, citing example after example of just how sick and perverted society has become, but that would simply be a waste of your time and mine. If you doubt that society is as sick as I say, all you need to do is go on the internet and read the lead stories on the welcome screen. Look at the headlines of your local newspaper. Look at the movies that are playing this week or the sit-coms that are on your TV tonight. You'll immediately realize that what I've said is absolutely true.

I was totally disgusted one night when I turned on the TV and watched the "monologue" of one of the more popular late night comedians.

His monologue ran for about 6 minutes I believe, and was just a litany of dirty moronic sex jokes one right after another. Every single line was about sex, boobs, orgasms, nudity, cheating, some part of the male anatomy, or mocking some "Christian nut-cake" who wanted to "get rid of pornography", mocking him for his "stupidity" and his "silly religion". And the audience just howled with laughter! I never heard one thing that was even remotely clever... it was just pure filth! (And this was the same "comedian" who actually spoke as if he believed in God back in September of 2001.)

I remember when Johnny Carson was the host of that show. In twenty years of watching his show, I never heard as much filth and garbage come out of his mouth as came out of this guys mouth in 6 minutes. What has happened to the soul of our once great nation?

Now... why should any of this even matter to you and me? Let me tell you why. Because I want to preserve this nation for my children and my grandchildren. I want it to be a place where they can live in peace and prosperity. And peace comes only from obedience to Gods laws.

If you'd like to know whether or not what I'm telling you about finding peace and happiness is true, take time yourself to read God's words from the Bible. If you do, you'll feel his spirit whisper to your soul that the things you see going on all around you are profoundly wrong and evil; these worldly perversions can never bring true happiness, not in this life, and definitely not in the next!

When are we as a nation going to finally have the courage to stand up and speak out against the perverts and reprobates who are so skillfully working to destroy our Christian nation? When are we going to take back the art world, the entertainment world, and the music world, making them once again reflect the values that true Christians should hold sacred?

Are we even going to try to affect real change in America, or are we simply going to continue on with the "status-quo", content to sit sanctimoniously on the sidelines and watch these perverts who are dominating our culture, occasionally being titillated and aroused yet rationalizing that we're just "social victims", and there's nothing we can actually do about it, washing our hands in Pilate's basin and drying our hands on Judas' robe?

Do you think for one moment that Jesus was kidding when he said...

"I know thy works, that thou art neither cold nor hot: I would thou wert cold or hot.

"So then because thou art lukewarm, and neither cold nor hot, I will spue thee out of my mouth."

(Revelations 3: 15-16)

Do we understand that principle? Do we appreciate what He's saying here? If you're unsure what it means, let me translate it for you into modern English...

"I expect you to take a stand on moral issues, one way or the other. You're either for me, or you're against me... there is no middle ground. And those of you who think you can remain neutral and still profess to be Christian with one foot in the Christ camp and the other foot in Babylon, listen up... I'm going to spit you out of my mouth."

I hope you understand the point I'm trying to get across here. If reading this makes you want to live your life in conformity with the teachings and principles of Christianity, then I've accomplished my purpose. If it only makes you mad at me, or you think that I'm just another religious nut who's totally out of touch with "reality", then this book was clearly not intended for you. This book was written for and will only be understood by those who believe that Christ actually lives and that his teachings are just as important, just as relevant for us today as they were for the people who lived during his mortal ministry.

Please don't misunderstand me, I love this country. Most of the people in it are great people, and I love to talk with them and enjoy the great life we as Americans enjoy... but the vast majority of "Christian America" has lost its way and been deceived by the so called "experts" and "authorities" of our time. The future of our nation is looking less encouraging every day.

I cringe when I turn on the TV or the internet and the headlines that jump out talk about the "Hollywood elite", and who's shacked up with who and what a wonderful thing it is and how the paparazzi will be watching with baited breath for the name of their next illegitimate child... then speculate about whether or not the parents will actually decide to wed, or will they just continue to live together in sin? But of course that's not considered important to most people since marriage is now considered "optional". (And they never actually use the words illegitimate or sin.)

Or, if you like more serious journalism, you can read about how the "experts" in "relationships" caution young women to "do their homework first before getting naked with their latest heart-throb". After all, you don't want to make a "mistake" when you're considering taking your "relationship to the next level"! (I've actually heard these exact quotes from "respected professionals" on television news shows!) Do all these buzz-words and catch-phrases annoy anyone else, or is it just me?

These people go to school, get PhD's in psychology and relationship counseling or whatever it is they assume makes them experts in condoning and orchestrating immorality, and then they gain credibility and the respect of the pseudo-intellectuals and the morally bankrupt crowd by being invited on Oprah, or Dr. Phil, or The View. And then the counsel these people give to people only makes things worse in the eyes of God, but America drinks it all up and thinks these immoral "experts" are actually great thinkers and gifted therapists. But here's a news flash...

Wickedness never is, never was and never will be happiness! Period! Does that sound "judgmental" to you? A bit closed-minded perhaps? I'm sorry, but if you really believe in Christianity, then you'll understand that true happiness comes from God! It comes as a result of living Gods laws and doing his will. How many times have you heard or read that God IS Love. Probably quite often; after all, it's in the Bible and it's still true today!

People generally don't understand that since all good emanates from God that *real* love and *real* happiness can only be achieved by living the principles Jesus taught.

Oh sure, people often say they're happy when they run around and get drunk, fornicate and so forth... but that's NOT true happiness... its Satan's counterfeit to happiness! And most people can't tell the difference in the heat of the moment because the feelings, the exhilaration, the rush are very similar... but nearly everyone can tell the difference when the party's over, the crowd has gone home, and their mind has had time to reflect on recent events.

When you wake up in the morning, and you regret what happened the night before... *that's not happiness.*

When you remember making a fool of yourself around your friends or hurting someone's feelings... *you can be sure that isn't happiness.*

When you find out from the doctor that you have an STD, or that you're going to have a baby and you're not even sure who the father is... *that can never be construed to be true happiness.*

It's not that difficult. You don't need a doctorate in anything to understand what happiness **is** or **is not**. You don't need money or position or even a superior I.Q. What you do need, is an understanding of Christ, who he is, his teachings, and what it is He expects of us since he's the one who sacrificed his life and paid for our sins individually... in order to save us all from death and hell.

On the other hand, when you wake up in the morning, next to your **spouse**, and you know you can trust this person with your most intimate secrets as well as everything of value you possess... *that's happiness.*

When you have fun with friends and family, and you wake up *without* a hangover, knowing that you have done nothing you need to be embarrassed about the night before... *that's happiness.*

When your child is born and you know that this child will have the advantages of being raised by a loving mother *and* father who love each other completely, who will teach him or her exactly what life is really all about, without fear that he or she might develop problems due to your sexual promiscuity or "indiscretions"... *that's true happiness.*

When your family works together, unselfishly to do all they can to make each other happy, and you grow old watching your children learn to love each other, help one another, and worship God, giving thanks to him for the bounties of life and for the personal assurance you have of a better life after this one... *that's happiness.*

When you go to bed at night and your children are out having fun with wholesome friends, and you're at peace because you know they'll be safe and not get involved with gangs or drugs or sex because you've taught them that it's wrong, not because you *think* it's wrong, but **because God has said that it's wrong**, and they *believe and respect his teachings... that's happiness.*

Too many of us go around blaming society for all the problems that plague our lives or the lives of your children.

I have no sympathy for parents who look for someone to blame or sue or prosecute when they send their "little girl" off on spring break to the bars in Aruba or some other party destination **unsupervised** and then act shocked and devastated when some pervert abducts and rapes or kills their "little girl".

My question to those kind of parents is simply this... What did you honestly expect would happen? This world is full of evil perverts and sexual predators! Surely you must have understood that! This can't be a surprise to anyone!

If you throw your child into the lions den, don't act surprised when the lions devour that child! I believe that parents who send their young irresponsible minor children into the world unsupervised, knowing the dangers that are out there... will be held accountable by God for what happens to them. I'm certain, that at the very least, they'll have to answer to God for gross parental stupidity and dereliction of duty!

Parents who allow and even encourage their children to run off and have a "good time" on spring break are, at the very least, extremely stupid, and probably evil. They send them off, *knowing* that their son or someone else's son is going to get drunk or high on drugs, sink to his lowest animal state, look for some easy mark to defile, and do things which are immoral and forbidden by God.

They *know* their daughter is probably going to be defiled by one of these jerks (or many of them) yet they allow it because they've been duped into believing that this is somehow a "right of passage"! And after all, everyone's doing it!

Often these irresponsible parents allow it because they did it themselves when they were young, and they simply chalk it up to "youthful indiscretions" or "sewing ones wild oats". Of course some "responsible parents" prepare their children "properly" by making sure that their child takes along condoms or pills so their little girl won't **really** get into "trouble".

If you are one of *those* kind of parents, there's something you need to understand... *getting pregnant is not the sin... **it's the result of the sin**... a sin that you encouraged! And God will hold you responsible and accountable for your part in it!*

And don't get angry at me and accuse me of being some insensitive sanctimonious right-wing religious freak... I simply understand what morality is, and I don't happen to believe it's all that difficult to teach a boy to keep his zipper zipped up! If anyone doesn't agree with that, then obviously they're a huge part of the problem.

You've probably seen on television a commercial from Trojan, showing a bar full of disgusting dirty pigs, (I mean the actual 4 legged snorting curly tailed pigs) trying to pick up on these scantily clad girls in a bar. The advertisers make us believe that the girls are "too smart" to jump into bed with just any "pig", so of course they turn them down. One of these pigs, however, remembers that in order to get a "classy girl", he must first purchase a condom from the vending machine in the back hall. So that's what he does and after he puts in his money and twists the knob, he's immediately transformed into a handsome young man, sexy and charming. He walks back to the room, the girl smiles at him and they head out the door. What a charming story.

But remember this... when all is said and done, the boy is still a pig, and the girl is still a slut, and the people at Trojan should be embarrassed and publicly condemned for encouraging sexual promiscuity and the corruption of our youth and society in general.

God's prepared a place for them as well, and it's NOT going to be in Heaven!

I hope you realize as I do, that in order to fix this problem we need to start with ourselves and our children first. We need to take responsibility for *our* actions, and for the actions of *our* children.

Don't be foolish enough to believe for one minute that just because some "professional" has a diploma hanging on his wall with a bunch of letters behind his or her name, that that makes them an expert on the subject of morality, propriety, inner peace or happiness. With liberals running the majority of the institutions of "higher learning" today, you need to understand one very important concept; garbage in... garbage out.

Many of our nation's student and teachers have been duped into believing that the things they hear and learn at our universities must be correct simply because some "respected professor" told them it was so... but we must be wiser than that. These so-called "respected professors" are the people spoken of in the Bible who are ... *"ever learning, but never coming to a knowledge of the truth"!* (See 2nd Timothy 3: 1-7)

If anything you learn or teach contradicts the principles or teachings Jesus Christ taught, you can know with absolute certainty that those teachings are wrong and evil!

If you really want to find happiness and fulfillment in your life, remember this... you won't find it by following the masses. Christ declared...

"Enter ye in at the strait gate: for wide is the gate, and broad is the way, that leadeth to destruction, and many there be which go in thereat:

Because strait is the gate, and narrow is the way, which leadeth unto life, and few there be that find it."

(St. Matthew 7: 13, 14)

Now, if you're not quite sure what *that* means, again, let me translate... "The overwhelming majority of people in America have jumped on this P.C. train headed for misery and regret because they're too lazy, apathetic or simply don't understand that it takes effort, faith and perseverance to catch the bus bound for heaven. And only those willing to pay God's price will be allowed to get on board." And that price is obedience to his commandments and conformity to His teachings. And the fare is not open to debate.

So it's up to you... make your choice and take a stand. But remember this... when you're brought to stand before God, to make an accounting of your deeds in this life, Christ will look deep into your soul, and you'll feel naked before his powerful gaze. There will be no excuses then, no rationalizations that will soften the guilt we'll all feel at that moment **IF** we've done anything less than our very best. We won't be able to utter some pathetic excuse like... "Well, I thought it was ok, 'cause Oprah said it was, or Dr. Ruth told me it was only natural, or everyone else was doing it and I didn't want to come across as a prude".

No, at that moment, none of those ridiculous excuses will hold water, because you'll know, as He already knows, that that pesky little voice you kept hearing in the back of your head telling you not to go down that path was actually His voice speaking to you, trying to warn you to stay away from sin, and you chose NOT to listen to Him. Trust me... that will not be happiness!

On the other hand, IF you choose to listen to that little voice, if you take the road less traveled... if you make the effort to swim upstream, when everyone else around you is floating downstream with the garbage of life, making their way towards the cesspool of sin and social acceptance, you'll be able to stand erect with head held high, look Christ squarely in the eye and unabashedly declare that you truly did your best... and THAT will be true happiness.

So what'll it be? Will you join the ranks of Christian soldiers and fight this war with us? Or will you throw in the towel and simply be content to float down "apathy creek"? It's up to you.

Remember, each of us has been given the great gift of agency, to choose for ourselves what we will do with our lives, and what we will believe in and fight for. **We are absolutely free to make our own choices in life, but we are NOT free to choose the consequences or the rewards of those choices!** God alone will determine our wages and assign us our eternal rewards!

He's purchased us with his blood, and rescued us from hell on the condition that we accept and confess him as our Lord and God, and at least make an honest effort to keep *all* His commandments... *not just the ones that are popular or convenient at the time.*

If we choose to follow him, we'll find joy and happiness more wonderful than we can imagine. If, however, we choose not to follow him, we'll have no one to blame but ourselves for the situation we'll find ourselves in for all of eternity. It's our decision... let us choose wisely.

CHAPTER ELEVEN

AMERICA'S ENERGY CRISIS

America's energy crisis is exactly like the global warming crisis. It's nonsense and it's fabricated in large part by liberals who can't stand to see folks like you and me driving around this country using cheap fuel.

Liberals have worked tirelessly for years in an attempt to curtail the use of oil in the U.S. by sanctimoniously proclaiming that they're the only ones concerned about the environment and the future of our planet and therefore have to control the oil industry to save the planet.

The sad part is that we've allowed these people to get a strangle-hold on our nation's natural resources because of our general apathy over those we send to Washington, and now it's nearly impossible for anyone with common sense to dislodge these bloodsuckers from their positions of power and authority.

Liberals couldn't be happier. They feel like they've accomplished with the phony "oil shortage", something that they've never been able to achieve before. They know they've finally succeeded in getting their hands around the throat of the American people, and are absolutely euphoric with the present situation, because it means that they can dictate more than ever before the way people like you and I move around this country. They can now make us grovel and beg for their help to solve this "crisis". Wake up people! What were we thinking when we allowed these politicians to get their hooks into our freedoms and our lives? When are we, the people, going to send a clear message to Washington that we're "mad as hell, and we're not going to take it any longer"?

If I had my way, I'd put term limits on every Congressman and every Senator in Washington. Twelve years is plenty of time for any politician to serve, and after that, they should be sent back home to get a real job where they can't continue to ferment and rot in the cesspool of corruption that has become Washington D.C!

We need men and women with fresh ideas, with a realistic pulse on the community they represent, to make good laws and revoke bad ones, and see that the will of the people is carried out.

We need to be more involved with our political system to make sure the politicians we elect represent us accurately, *and then go home*!

It was Plato who said ... *"One of the penalties for refusing to participate in politics is that you end up being governed by your inferiors."* That has never been more true or more evident than it is today. Just look at the dysfunctional Congress and Senate now in session.

You see, one of the problems with career politicians in D.C. is that they live high on the hog, they rub shoulders with famous people, they have thousands of people clamoring for their attention, and so before long, they actually start to believe they're superior to everyone else, especially those they represent. But here's a NEWS FLASH for you politicians... you're just the hired help! And the people you work for are just as important as you are!

Politicians have largely forgotten that although they may live in a fancy hotel, condo or mansion and have some chauffeur drive them anywhere they want to go, most of the people they represent don't live that way!

They've forgotten that just because they might walk to work each day, or take a cab or public transportation of some sort, most of their constituents don't have that luxury! Most of us have to drive vehicles that use GAS, and at $4.00 per gallon, it's killing us along with many of our hopes and dreams! Many of us, those of us who pay taxes and make this nation run, live in rural America, with real jobs, making products and building things, and our jobs are not two blocks away in an air-conditioned office building! Our jobs are often hundreds of miles away, and all of our profits are being eaten up by rising gas prices!

These "elite" politicians arrogantly thumb their noses at suggestions on how to make this nation energy independent, because they imagine themselves to be "so much more intelligent" than we are. They won't allow us to develop nuclear power which is clean and cheap and widely used throughout the world because they have this superior vision of an America that uses "alternative energies" that are safe, and "green"! Really? What are they? Where are they?

We need to dust off the drills and start punching new holes in the ground immediately to avert an all out melt-down of the economy and the American way of life.

We need to build new oil refineries NOW, and we need to open up ANWR and the coastal oil fields immediately!

We need to build nuclear reactors ASAP and get them online, and ignore all the whining and protests from the green freaks and libs who argue that this type of energy is simply "too dangerous"!

America has a great safety record when it comes to nuclear reactors. The anti-nuclear crowd point out that even one death would be too many. How many people die each year as a result of drunk driving, or drugs, or slipping and falling in their own homes?

Why do WE THE PEOPLE allow corrupt politicians to sit around in Washington and fester and become corrupt while we sit at home helpless to get them to do the things that ordinary intelligent people instinctively know needs to be done?

When are the arrogant politicians in Washington going to give the go-ahead to start producing oil from the shale we have in the Rocky Mountain States? Who exactly are these elite people who think the oil industry is so stupid that they can't intelligently extract the oil from oil-shale and convert it to oil without "destroying the environment"?

It's people in Washington who don't have to make an "honest" living like you and me that are the real problem. They're the ones who don't understand what's really going on. They have no empathy for the little guy who's struggling to make ends meet. They just sit back there in Washington, drinking and laughing, slapping each other on the back as they pass more useless legislation, laws, idiotic regulations and restrictions that work to cripple and hog-tie this country and its entrepreneurs.

We need to repeal some of the ridiculous wilderness restrictions that are killing our economy, and start using the resources God's prepared and provided for us to use. And we can do that in a respectful and responsible way!

I was flabbergasted one day when I heard some liberal lady back east saying that we in America had no right to have access to cheap oil. She argued, that "Americans ought to pay just as much for gas as any of the European nations have to pay, because "we're no better then they are."

What kind of logic is that? This is leftist logic at its worst! First of all, I don't care how much Europeans pay for gas; I only care about how much WE as Americans have to pay for OUR gas. Liberals like this woman don't understand that most of the people in Europe live in or near large cities with mass transit systems already in place to move people around. Many of their citizens don't even OWN a car, and hardly anyone owns a pick-up truck. But here's a news flash for anyone who buys into that shtick... *We are not Europe!* Our states are bigger than most of their countries and most people in rural America have to drive miles to get to work, or go to stores, or visit relatives, and in most places, there are no trains, no busses and no subways! You simply cannot compare the U.S. to Europe!

If some people think America ought to pay the same price for gas as Europeans do, then why don't they do the honorable thing... let them pay the oil companies eight or nine bucks a gallon, and let the rest of us pay two bucks a gallon. That way, they're happy, we're happy, and they can feel like they're really doing their part. If they don't like that solution, then by all means, they should feel free to move to Europe and pay through the nose for all their gas! I'll even be happy to throw them a going-away party!

Meanwhile, give this nation back it's dreams, get us energy independent, and let us get back to doing what we do best as a nation, which is inventing things, building things, and improving the quality of life for everyone on the planet!

The federal Government needs to get out of the way of business and quit trying to force ridiculous regulations and their "green technology" ideas on us. Government is a disaster when it comes to job creation.

This nation, with Gods help, has done more to lift and improve the life and lifestyles of the people on this planet than any other nation in its history. We've freed captive nations; we've rescued countries from evil dictators and war-lords; we've saved and healed millions upon millions of people throughout the world with our medicine, our charities, and our technologies; we've raised the standard of living for billions of people around the world, and we've asked nothing in return.

When we've found it necessary to go to war, we have NOT plundered and taken over the nations we conquered, but have rebuilt and liberated them, making it possible for them to become great and independent as well, even assisting them with money and technology so they could reach their full potential!

Yet with all this, the liberals and the America haters somehow feel that we are this "Evil Empire" that needs to pay penance for how we've corrupted the world. Well I have news for you. I don't believe America owes anyone an apology.

We're not perfect, but we're a whole lot better than the rest of the nations in this world who achieved super-power status. Name one nation that has done as much good for humanity! Which nation does more to defend freedom? Which nation is more admired by the world? Why do so many want to come here to live? And which nation does the entire world look to for leadership and protection?

I hope every person in this country will take a serious look at their elected leaders, and if they're not for drilling here and NOW, if they aren't fighting for energy independence, we need to kick their butts out of Washington the first chance we get!

We have so many people in Washington telling us we need "alternative energy" to save the planet, but not one of those people actually has a clue what that "alternative" might be!

They want to use corn for fuel, but that is seriously stupid. It's inefficient, costly, takes food out of the mouths of starving people, ties up fertile farmland and it's driven by political correctness rather than intelligence.

If they really want to get involved and give people incentive to improve our energy technologies, they should offer One Billion Dollars to the person or company that actually discovers a viable alternative energy source. Aside from that, they should stay out of the way!

We can and should be searching for new solutions and new technology for the future, and we ought to be doing that right now... but in the meantime, let's not hang this nation out to dry! This is not just an issue of transportation; it's a serious security threat!

But most of the bureaucrats in Washington don't really care about the security of this nation. They only care about personal power and position. They honestly think that they're smarter than we are, that they are God's gift to humanity, sent here to save this planet from bumpkins like you and me.

These arrogant elitists actually believe that this planet can't survive without their help. Never mind the fact that this world has been spinning around for... what did Carl Sagan say... "billions of years", and now, somehow, the "ugly Americans" are going to put it out of business in a matter of just a few short years!

How ridiculous does that sound? Do you really believe that God is so inept, so short-sighted, that he would create a planet for his children to live on, supply them with resources and knowledge about how to harness those resources, and then allow them to destroy themselves because they weren't careful enough with the resources he's given us?

I know libs and atheists will rant that God isn't the issue here... that conservation and intelligence are the issues. But remember... many of these "geniuses" are people who don't believe in a God. Or these are people who don't trust God. These are people who actually believe they're smarter than God, "if there is one", and their self-proclaimed destiny is to "save the planet"! Give me a break!

The truth is that these are arrogant, opportunistic elitists who have their own personal agendas and don't give a hoot about truth or facts unless those facts happen to support their point of view.

I'm tired of talking about all the problems this country has. I'm sick of politicians who don't care about us "little people". I'm sick of the liberal elitists who think the average American is an idiot. I'm fed up with the ACLU, the "gay-rights" advocates, the special interest groups who put money and profits ahead of God and country. I'm tired of Godless Americans who are trying to muzzle the Christian masses and push their amoral agendas down our throats. And if you've had enough of these people as well, then join with me in starting a grass roots effort to take back America!

It's time to reaffirm that this nation is indeed a Christian nation, (in spite of what Obama says) and we want to have our voices heard!

It's time to put our trust in that God who created and preserved this great nation specifically for "we the people" so that we could become that shining city on the hill for the rest of the world to look to for leadership in every important aspect of life.

I know there are people who will disagree fiercely with the things I've written. That's fair enough. After all... it's still a free country... a free Christian country. And I'm free to disagree with them. But it is a fact that this nation has achieved heights no nation in the history of this planet has ever achieved, and it's precisely because this nation was founded by God-fearing Christians that it's risen to the stature and prominence it enjoys today.

This nation is the greatest nation ever to grace this planet, but it's by no means a status that's guaranteed to remain if the people of this nation turn their backs on that God who made it all possible. In fact, quite the opposite is true. When the time comes that the majority of the people choose evil instead of good, when they choose sin, corruption and decadence over humility, repentance and worship of the true and living God; when they choose murder and abortion and pornography over life and love and chastity, then God will withdraw his protection and his blessings. And that God who has heretofore preserved and protected us will open the floodgates of his chastisements upon us, and there will be no military powerful enough, no fortifications strong enough, and no weapons potent enough to protect the people of this land.

We must always remember; **"If God be for us, who can be against us?"** But the opposite is also true. **"If God be against us,**

we're SOL!" (I'm not exactly sure *where* that can be found in the Bible, but I'm sure it's true just the same.)

As for the so call "energy crisis", that argument is losing its credibility more and more each day as scientists, explorers and oil companies discover more and more huge pockets of oil, natural gas, and cleaner coal. Yes, I'm confident that there are green technologies that one day will be discovered that will be much better for all of us, but we haven't discovered them yet and until we do, we can't afford to back up and re-enter the dark ages simply to accommodate the liberals who are trying to destroy America.

Some folks think I'm too hard on liberals, arguing that they want America to succeed just as much as I do... they just have a different path they think is better. Call me cynical, but I don't believe it. I think many of these liberals really are evil. I think they despise America and they despise God.

I believe they won't rest until they destroy this country's "exceptionalism", and pull us down to match the moral mediocrity of the rest of the world. We must never allow that to happen.

CHAPTER TWELVE

WHEN NEWS IS **NOT** NEWS

When I was a kid, you could go to virtually any of the three major news networks and get pretty much the same information. The NEWS that was reported was just that... news. The only thing that made people prefer one news organization over another, were the personalities, the anchors, sportscasters or weathermen.

Today however, news isn't really news anymore. Today, the "news" is bloviating, it's partisan posturing, it's manipulation of the "facts" to further the agenda of liberal organizations who for one reason or another have forgotten what real news is supposed to be. They're not interested in the truth, only in being able to engineer the story to steer people's thinking in a direction that furthers their personal agenda.

I looked up news in the dictionary, and this is what it said...

News 1. a: a report of recent events b: previously unknown information 2 a: material reported in a newspaper or news periodical or on a newscast b: matter that is newsworthy.

By definition then, I contend that the "news" of today, is at best, not news at all, but opinion and social engineering.

The liberal "newscasters" of today couch their words and their stories in such a way as to lead and influence the "listener" in the direction they want them to go. Rarely are the "facts" factual at all, but instead are manipulations to push the not so subtle agenda of the person or network "reporting" the "news".

The major networks we once relied on for truth and accuracy have now become video tabloids who have sold their journalistic souls to the devil of political correctness.

Newscasters ought to at least have the integrity to report the news, keeping it unbiased and accurate allowing viewers to draw their own conclusions. And if they have strong feelings on it one way or the other, they should at least have the honesty to admit that what they're saying is opinion, commentary or political spin. But obviously that is not going to happen.

Liberals don't want the truth because it undermines their efforts to control and manipulate others to advance their agenda.

It's for these and many other reasons that truth and morality are in decline. One of the most powerful forces in the world today is peer pressure. That's nothing new. Peer pressure has always been a powerful force... for good or evil. And it all depends on where the people are at the time. Unfortunately, the pendulum has swung from good and spiritual to evil and secular over the past 40 years. What that means is this...

We're at a moment in the history of this Nation when it's not cool to be religious. Our social Icons are morally bankrupt, our leaders are generally corrupt, and the pervasive attitude of the population is one of apathy or even open hostility when it comes to matters of faith and religion. People who claim to be followers of a particular faith are often critical of the doctrine of their Church and it's leaders because they don't like the idea of absolutes in their lives. Let me give you an example.

President Obama said for years that his views on marriage have been that "marriage is between one man and one woman." That was his stance in 2008 when it was the popular opinion to espouse. Now, people have become more radical, more secular, more "tolerant" of the media-driven homosexual agenda, and so he has now reversed course. He now says that he's "evolved" in his thinking, and has publicly declared his support *for* "gay marriage". And the news media and the liberal socialists praise his "evolution", heaping ridicule and criticism on anyone who has a different point of view.

So now the main-stream-media is under orders to attack ruthlessly anyone who doesn't agree with Obama's new found "enlightened position", impugning their character and destroying the lives of anyone who disagrees with him, never giving a second thought to minor details like truth, logic, reality or most importantly... what does God say about it.

And that's the big problem... because we **already** know what God has to say about it... and we know... because God IS God. He's the same today, yesterday, and forever. His commandments are unchanging which means that his commandments that have been in force for many thousands of years, are still in force today. You see, unlike Obama, God is not "evolving"! God NEVER evolves... because he's already PERFECT! The only way perfection can change, is to become "imperfect", at which point, God would cease to be God. Who in this world, calling themselves "Christians" can be so stupid as to believe that God will change his views on marriage and morality simply because a bunch of leftist imperfect people think it would be nice to be more tolerant?

The fact of the matter is that God has already repudiated and condemned the sin of homosexuality, and therefore anyone who is *for* "gay marriage" is taking a position that is squarely against God. It really is just that simple.

But this President is a panderer. He appears to have no solid moral convictions... only a finger-to-the-wind philosophy.

Honest, descent statesmen in this day and age are few and far between. It's easy to find talented orators who have the charisma and charm to wow the populace and manipulate their minds into following them wherever they want them to go. But it's nearly impossible to find decent God-fearing statesmen who have our nation's best interest and the good of the people and the nation at heart.

History will one day attest to the fact that Ronald Reagan was one of the greatest presidents this nation has ever had. Here was a man who cared about what God thought, not what was politically correct or expedient at the time. Here was a man who truly had the good of the people at the forefront of his agenda, instead of lining his pockets with the hard earned money of those he served. Here was a man who took on the left-wing Caucasus of congress and the media, yet was able to spar with them pleasantly, and in such a way as to sway and persuade many of them to join him and his cause. (Actually, if they bucked him, he just took his case to the people, and *they* pressured their elected officials to join him or face the consequences at the polls!)

When President Reagan was elected, the liberals in Washington suffered a severe setback in their nefarious scheme to take over Washington and promote their liberal ideas. It galled them that this unsophisticated "outsider" could come in and boldly, brashly and unapologetically undermine their socialist aspirations. But Reagan was so powerful, so persuasive and charismatic with the "common folk", that all they could do was to pull back and hope he would eventually go away. He did, but not until he had proven that his views on the economy, taxes and the cold war were correct! He crushed communism in many parts of the world, and brought freedom and prosperity to many others.

Today, we're once again faced with decisions that will impact America for generations to come. We've elected the most liberal Democrat this nation's ever seen to the highest office in the land. This is a man who despises the very military that's kept and preserved his freedoms. Here's a man who says his belief in God is very important in his life, yet he rarely attends church, and he voted against a law that would have saved little babies who survived "botched" abortions. That doesn't sound like a man who's found Jesus.

If a person took a newborn puppy, put it into a burlap sack and threw it into the river, he would be derided, demonized, ostracized and prosecuted to the fullest extent of the law. Animal rights activists would call for his head on a platter! Liberals would milk the story for all it's worth, particularly if that puppy-killer was a conservative or a Republican... yet they absolutely refuse to admit or recognize that ignoring a crying human baby, struggling to stay alive in some abortion clinic or hospital is *infinitely* worse, *infinitely more repugnant and evil* in the eyes of God than drowning some puppy!

If that's the kind of treatment that Obama's GOD approves of, I want no part of his God. That sounds exactly like the God of the Islamo-terrorists... a god who condones the killing of innocent babies to further some radical agenda. Obama says he's not

Muslim, yet supporting infanticide is absolutely, positively NOT a Christian doctrine!

If you believe that God will simply look the other way or somehow excuse the doctors, nurses and others involved in this type of *murder*, you do not understand who or what God is! (Yes... refusing to save a baby by allowing it to starve, or by killing it with drugs or suffocation or scrambling its brains *is* murder.)

I wonder if our founding fathers ever imagined that one day this great nation, the nation they pledged their lives, their fortunes and their sacred honor to bring about, would be fighting for its very soul... not on the battlefield of war, but in the minds and hearts of every American citizen.

Liberals want to "reinvent" this nation, trashing the lofty ideas and ideals that made this nation what it is today: the greatest nation on earth, the beacon of freedom and democracy in a world of corrupt governments.

I say, if the liberals and the so-called progressives of this nation hate America so much, by all means, pack your bags and leave! Go to France or the Netherlands or wherever it is on this earth you believe is so much better than this nation; and be sure to write.

Go and live your life of liberalism, thumbing your collective noses at the God of Christianity, and when you and your ilk find yourself in the position of being murdered and overrun by some evil dictator or religious fanatic who declares war on your newfound "fatherland", don't look to America to save your butts!

I'm sick and tired of the character assassins and the political pit-bulls these liberal folk sic on people who are trying to preserve this nation and its glorious Christian traditions!

Sarah Palin was such a breath of fresh air! Here was a woman who demonstrated she had the courage to stand up against the "good-old-boys" of corrupt politics and the business-as-usual politicians who are destroying this nation. But instead of gratitude for her patriotism, she's been demonized by the liberals and the left wing crazies.

If that act alone isn't enough to demonstrate to sane people just how corrupt and evil the left has become, I don't know what is.

Here is a woman... a woman, who you would think the bra-burning feminist babes of this nation would embrace and praise for finally elevating women to the same heights and status of men, but instead of rejoicing, they ridicule and deride her because she's too "conservative".

The feminists of this country absolutely hate Sarah Palin. They hate her because she looks good, and has intelligence. They hate her because she has the audacity to wear a dress and pack a gun. They despise her because she has the courage to confess a belief in God openly, and refused to kill her unborn baby just because he wasn't going to be "normal"!

These "ladies" (and I use the term very loosely) hate her because she believes that the American dream can be achieved by honest hard work, without embracing the radical, hateful agenda of left-wing Socialists.

They, as well as the rest of the left-wing liberals absolutely HATE this woman because she IS "Reaganesque"!

This is a woman who is strong, likable, intelligent, persuasive, and attractive! In short, this woman scares the heck out of the left. They were afraid that if this woman was allowed to succeed, it would have set back liberalism and the feminist movement twenty years.

This they COULD NOT have, and so they did everything in their power to destroy her.

Sarah had her hands full, especially when you consider she not only had to take on the corrupt politicians, the liberal elite and the feminazis, but she also had to take on the entire "mainstream" media!

I heard a report on the radio one day during the elections of 2008, where one of the more prominent and respected news show personalities said the following when asked why he and the "mainstream" media were being so brutal to Sarah Palin ... He said... "It's our job to dig up dirt on the candidates".

This is how screwed-up these "journalists" have become. But I notice they *never* "dig up dirt" on the liberal socialist candidates... why is that? It's called a double standard... it's called hypocrisy.

The really disturbing thing about this idiotic statement is this:

These people say that they are just "doing their duty" to try and uncover and expose any and all dirt on the candidates. Yet they'd known for two years that Obama had close, even intimate dealings with convicted felons, terrorists, America-haters and people of the worst kind, yet they not only refused to examine his relationships with these people, but in most cases either ignored the facts or tried to vilify the person sharing the information. (Kill the messenger!)

The ultimate irony and hypocrisy of their position, is this:

John F. Kennedy, in their minds, is right up there next to God in greatness and Democrat veneration. Just the mention of his name causes most of these Libs to have hot flashes, (or send tingles up the inside of Chris Matthews's legs.) Yet if anyone had exposed a hundredth part of the real "dirt" John F. Kennedy was hiding in his closet, he could never have gotten elected garbage collector, let alone President of the United States. None of the Kennedy clan would have ever been remembered for any great accomplishments, except maybe that they were S.O.B.s (sons of a bootlegger.)

Yet here was a woman of great moral character and superior governing experience when compared with Obama, and the attack dogs searched for every thing they could possibly find in order to trip her up or cause her to pull out of the race.

These "news people" are hypocrites of the first order! These are the same folks who whined and complained about the Republicans when they brought up Bill Clintons shenanigans in the White House, protesting that "moral issues had no bearing on his ability to lead as president!" But that, of course, was never the issue, and they knew it. The issue was the fact that he'd screwed around on the job, and then perjured himself under oath, and tried to cover it up! Hillary knew what was going on, but she tried to deflect the negative attention by crying that it was "all part of some vast right-wing conspiracy!"

Sarah Palin survived all their attacks, and they still wouldn't let her alone. She's still a thorn in their side that just won't go away... and this is what drives them crazy. Bigots and hate-mongers on the left will stop at nothing to destroy and discredit her because she represents the biggest threat these people have seen in the past thirty years!

So here we are. The big question is this... are we going to continue down the path of moral bankruptcy and crony capitalism, or are we going to change direction and put people into office who are honest in their business dealings and who love the old style Democracy that America is known for?

Are we going to continue down the path of socialism, welfare dependence, class warfare, racial division, and backroom deals, or are we going to put a President in who understands the meaning of honesty, integrity, and openness?

Are we going to continue on with this experiment that we've been conducting the past few years of having a "rock-star" in the White House who knows nothing of business, foreign affairs, the economy or how to inspire people to excel and succeed in their personal lives?

Are we going to continue to have scandal after scandal in our government, with rampant immorality, reckless spending, wasteful budgets, and ridiculous experimentation on "green energies" or are we going to put an adult in the White House who will restore dignity, honesty, openness, respect and leadership in America and abroad? The choice is up to you.

CHAPTER THIRTEEN

IN CONCLUSION

If anyone's wondering why I felt the urge to sit down and write this book, let me explain...

First of all, I'm saddened and very much concerned with the direction our country is headed. I'm fed-up with all the politically correct nonsense that's perverted and emasculated the English language. It's destroying the real America; the America that once demanded and deserved the respect of the entire free world. I'm sick and tired of Libs and social elitists vilifying our American heroes... "real" men and women who once demanded respect and admiration, replacing them instead with a bunch of hand picked left wing namby-pambies who insist on everyone being "tolerant" and "sensitive".

A military officer, a close friend of mine who's served his whole life in the Army Air Corps and has been deployed several times to the Middle East, told me of a meeting of many of the worlds most powerful military leaders who had gathered together to discuss recent events and the military conflicts going on around the world. During the discussion, a Frenchman spoke up and asked... "Why is it that whenever we assemble to discuss these issues we must always speak English?"

Now I'm sure that that's precisely the kind of question liberals and "intellectuals" would like to ask as well. Anything to embarrass the "ugly Americans".

Well, the question was actually answered by a British officer who was forthright and candid in his reply. He simply looked at this condescending Frenchman and replied... "Because YOU lost the bloody war!"

America has shown time and time again, that its character, its personality, its daring and courage are precisely what are needed in this dangerous world to preserve and defend the principles of democracy and freedom whenever and wherever necessary.

I for one love the fact that much of the world looks on us as a nation of "cowboys", bold, brave, brash and unrefined. I loved John Wayne! He was a man, not a sissy! Hollywood could use about ten thousand more John Wayne's.

On the other hand, liberals want us to be more like the Europeans, to accept their philosophies and change our culture to mimic theirs. But that's not who we are and hopefully we never will be!

Who in their right mind would want the United States to resemble France, the Netherlands, Germany, Sweden or any other European nation?

We are US... the U.S. of A! And if that's so bad, then why are people by the thousands flocking to our shores, trying to break down our fences to get into our country every single day? I don't believe we need to apologize for being the greatest nation on earth and I was especially irritated when Obama went on his apology tour.

I believe this country IS exceptional... and one of the things that make us so exceptional is our dedication to preserving freedom and democracy not just for ourselves but for all freedom loving people around the world. What's wrong with that?

Why is it that liberals who live in America can't see this great nation for what it is? Why do they want to marginalize and homogenize it to resemble the very nations that have become second rate powers and third rate societies?

We cannot, we must not prostitute ourselves and our country simply to "fit in" with the rest of the world! Europe has basically sold its soul to the devil, denying God and relegating religion to little more than outdated old-fashioned folk-lure, an antiquated idea that's been outgrown by the elite and only occasionally practiced by the "mentally feeble and superstitious".

America is the greatest nation ever inhabited by man for one reason... because *God designed it to be so*. He raised up great men and women with great minds and remarkable character specifically to bring about the birth of this amazing nation. His Spirit still broods over her, inspiring men and women to fight for truth and right. He wants us to understand that true Christian principles will never be outdated. Belief in God will always make men and nations stronger, not weaker; better, not worse.

Maintaining a moral compass is our only hope for America. If we give in to the corruption and the moral decadence the world now embraces, we'll find ourselves in the exact same situation as all the other nations who have rejected God, and our fate will ultimately be the same.

It's not just important, it's absolutely *vital* that we remember the past, because the past provides us with a window to our future.

When I was a small boy, I loved December 7th. The reason I loved it was because every year on that day, the entire day was devoted to remembering and honoring the men and women killed at Pearl Harbor. There were always war shows on TV on that day, with the likes of John Wayne, Henry Fonda, Charlton Heston, Robert Mitchum and a multitude of other movie stars who proudly displayed their patriotism, both on screen and off.

Today however, things are very different. The geniuses of the media have determined that it's inappropriate to show that horrific day in 2001. They've decided it's not good for our children, or for those who lost loved ones on that day to be reminded of that "tragic" event. "There's no reason to dig up those awful feelings of anger and hurt. It's better to just leave it alone and move on with life. No good can come by stirring up the memories of that horrible day"... so they say.

But they don't care about the feelings of the victims. They aren't concerned about the children, or the country healing, or the division it might cause between people of different ethnic backgrounds.

The only reason they hate being reminded of that day and the only reason they refuse to allow it to be viewed by the American public, is because they know, that if Americans are reminded of that horrific act of terror often enough, it will affect the way they think and the way they vote, and consequently, the leaders they put into office. They know that when America remembers the evil attacks of that day, they are much more likely to vote for Presidents who are Republicans, who love this country and are proud of it, and who will do whatever is necessary to protect and preserve this nation's freedoms and traditions. When people are reminded of the past, they remember what makes this nation great, and they look for people with the same qualities our founding fathers had; men who will work hard to keep this nation unique, powerful and free.

These leftists are hugely hypocritical! If they thought for one minute that the vision of those towers crumbling to the ground would garner them votes, or further their agenda, they'd begin every newscast with it.

But liberals know that's not the case, so they won't allow that to happen. They want us to believe that the best way to handle this "tragedy" is to beef up security in all our airports and take away more of our freedoms.

These geniuses feel that the best way to keep us safe is to strip-search all the grandmas and children who may or may not look suspicious. They intimidate and interrogate every person who has the nerve to go to the airport with a suspicious prosthetic, or an unfamiliar catheter bag, and they do all this so they don't look like they're "profiling" the people who actually DO fit the profile of the terrorists who attacked America.

The politicians and government workers of this country have gone insane! But let me get back to the real threat facing America.

History has a way of repeating itself; it's one of the laws of nature. And we only deceive ourselves if we think for one moment that we can travel down the same corrupt road as nations past, and somehow arrive at a different destination. If we dishonor God, we forfeit his blessings. If we break his commandments, we set ourselves up for destruction, whether by man, or by God himself, *it doesn't matter... the results will be the same.*

Man, the "enlightened natural man", will of course think that this is simply rubbish and superstition, that God is nothing more than a crutch for the simple minded and uneducated. And this ignorant arrogant attitude will undoubtedly remain and even increase in our nation until Christ comes to begin his reign on Earth, or until some other catastrophic event occurs to humble the American people and drive them once again to their knees.

I don't know when that will occur, but this much I can promise you: *The day will come when you and I, all of us who claim to be Christians, as well as every other person who has ever lived on this earth, regardless of who they've chosen or invented to worship as Deity, will have to stand before Jesus Christ, and then he will demand an accounting from each of us... our actions, our words, and our deeds.*

At that time, it will be too late for "Christians" to declare whose side they're on. God will already know, and so will we.

The only question that remains for you and me is this... Do we have the courage to stand up for what's right **today**? Will we have the courage to stand firm with all true believing, *practicing* Christians who have the courage of their convictions and the will to take a stand against the pernicious evils and polluted philosophies of the so called intellectual elite and the "progressive Christians"?

Can we be strong in standing up against the unbelievers and the "sell-outs" who claim to be Christian when it suits their needs, then rationalize and intellectualize Gods teachings when it's no longer politically expedient?

Will we have the courage to stand for Christ, to teach our children that morality isn't outdated, nor is it relative? Will our children understand that patriotism and honor are just as important today as they were two hundred years ago?

Where do you stand? I hope you make the decision to stand with me, and with every other Christian who truly believes in God.

When I was a child, I stood up every day at the beginning of the school day and with the rest of my classmates proudly repeated the pledge of allegiance. I believe every child in every school should continue that practice today. It's a way to honor those who have died to give us this free country we live in today.

And if we pledge allegiance to the flag and to our nation... what would be so wrong with pledging allegiance to Christ, to his teachings, and his principles? Not in a public arena, but on a personal basis. What would be so wrong with taking a pledge to actually live the Ten Commandments that Christ's given us?

If we'd all make that pledge, and really mean it, there would be little need for all the millions of laws that clutter the bookshelves of our nations courts and capitols. The 10 commandments, if honestly accepted and obeyed, would eliminate the need for about 90 percent of our lawyers, judges, policemen, jails, penitentiaries, homeless shelters, soup kitchens, drug rehabs, hospitals, detention centers, and a host of other programs and policies that exist because of the evils of a godless society.

In reality, many of us do take that pledge... most of us just don't realize it. Isn't that the pledge we take when we go to church and confess that Jesus is the Christ? Isn't that the pledge we make when we partake of communion or sacrament or attend confession? Don't we re-affirm our personal commitment to Jesus, his teachings and his commandments in those moments? Isn't it about time that we as a nation have the courage to stand up and say to the liberals and socialists who are trying to destroy this

"Christian" nation that *enough is enough, and we're not going to let that happen*?

We absolutely need to elect people who'll begin the ominous task of getting rid of big government and allowing people to live productive lives by actually building or creating things that will make this world and this nation a better place.

We need to get rid of the ridiculous mountains of regulations that take away our freedoms and discourage entrepreneurship. We need to work to eliminate the jobs of those who act as "big brother" looking over our shoulders to make sure that we are doing all the preposterous little details these meddling politicians have invented to make our lives more restrictive and miserable.

It's time for a national resurgence of religion, to push back the Anti-Christ-Litigation-Union and become free once again to speak our minds without fear of being destroyed by God hating liberals and socialists.

It's time to make America great once again, and realize that the path we're on is the same liberal path that every great nation throughout history found themselves going down just prior to their demise. History has demonstrated that secular progressive liberal thinking ALWAYS leads to the same results... the corruption and destruction of civilization.

My goal is to get as many people as I can to read this book and act on the truths it contains. I believe that if just one percent of the American population would read and do the things I've suggested in this book, which is to re-commit to being a "practicing Christian", not just a "closet Christian", we would change not only the course of this nation, but the destiny of the entire world! We MUST take a stand and let others know where we stand, ***especially our own*** *children.* We need to let others know that we do believe in Christ, that we accept him as our Savior, that following his teachings and examples makes us stronger, not weaker, and it makes us better citizens of this great nation!

President Obama and nearly the entire Democratic party recently declared that they are now firmly for "gay marriage". What a travesty! Do these arrogant politicians and leftist liberals actually believe that they can mock God, that they can effectively "veto" the teachings in the Bible and that this will somehow pressure God into changing his basic laws of morality?

The ignorance of their position is punctuated by their explanations as to "why" they feel they must come to the defense of those who reject and mock Christ's teachings.

Obama said that it was his "faith" that ultimately made him change his thinking, and "evolve" in his views causing him to finally embrace the homosexual agenda. Liberals embraced his new-found conviction and declared his "evolution" as "courageous". Nonsense. There's nothing courageous about caving in to evil and turning your back on Christ and his teachings. This President knows full well that *real* courage would only be demonstrated if he had the guts to stand firmly on the Lord's side... the side of truth and right and morality... in spite of the ridicule and criticism of leftist social terrorists.

True courage *demands* that people stand up for morality, even when they know that the hate-mongers on the left will do all they can to crucify them for criticizing immorality! Remember... they crucified Christ for similar reasons... but He refused to cave in!

Real Christians... intelligent Christians, understand this one simple concept...

Morality, the Ten Commandments, the teachings of Christ, the principles and truths contained in the Bible are the foundation of correct thinking and action for all people in all ages! God established these principles as the FOUNDATION of his doctrine. *Foundations were never intended to bend or break or become weak over time... that is NOT what foundations are designed to do! And God will never modify his commandments to accommodate sin or the opinions of the spiritually ignorant.*

Men demonstrate their arrogance and ignorance when they announce that they simply cannot accept the "old fashioned" traditions and morality that God expected of his followers because it "doesn't make sense" in today's world.

Perhaps they need to read the Bible a little more carefully. They may begin to realize that as God says...

"For my thoughts are not your thoughts, neither are your ways my ways, saith the Lord.

"For as the heavens are higher than the earth, so are my ways higher than your ways, and my thoughts than your thoughts." (Isaiah 55:8-9)

When will puny arrogant man finally realize that we're not remotely equivalent to God either intellectually or morally? Only when we as humans have the humility to recognize and admit our own ignorance, will we start to gain real intelligence.

Several prominent "Christian" churches in the United States have caved in to political correctness and removed many of the traditional Hymns from their Hymnals, declaring them to be "divisive" or "hateful" or "polarizing". Hymns like Onward Christian Soldiers", or "We are All Enlisted" have been removed because they speak of "war" and "enemies", "good" and "evil", "fighting" and "conquering". But the fact is... **WE ARE AT WAR!** Listen to the words of the Apostle Paul in the Bible...

"For we wrestle not against flesh and blood, but against principalities, against powers, against the rulers of the darkness of this world, <u>against spiritual wickedness in high places</u>.

Werefore take unto you the whole armour of God, that ye may be able to withstand in the evil day, and having done all, to stand.

Stand therefore, having your loins girt about with truth, and having on the breastplate of righteousness;

And your feet shod with the preparation of the gospel of peace;

Above all, taking the shield of faith, wherewith ye shall be able to quench all the fiery darts of the wicked.

And take the helmet of salvation, and the sword of the Spirit, which is the word of God."

Ephesians 6: 12 – 17

Yes... we are at war. And when Paul spoke of "spiritual wickedness in high places", he was speaking specifically and directly to religious leaders who rationalize and water down Christ's teachings in order to maintain popularity with the people. (Pandering to the masses.) He was describing today's religious leaders who betray Christ and dismiss morality as old fashioned. (Morality is ALWAYS in fashion.) He was speaking of pastors and preachers who cave in to political correctness and leftist secularism. (Because they need their monetary assistance.) He was speaking also of political leaders who _claim_ to be Christians as they attempt to garner the "Christian vote", then thumb their noses at Christ's doctrine and commandments so they don't incur the wrath of liberals and homosexuals.

I'm flabbergasted when I hear so called Christian ministers and clergy argue that Christ's views on homosexuality are simply outdated, even arguing that "Christ _would_ support gay marriage today because He also supported the golden rule". Do they really have the audacity, the _arrogance_ to question God's intelligence and his resolve regarding this principle, replacing it with perverted logic, sinful rationalizations and pseudo-Christianity?

We absolutely _are_ at war... a war that will determine the future of the United States, and define the very soul of America far into the next century. Will we have the courage to fight this war in spite of the hate and hypocrisy of the left, or will we lose this war and join forces with the misguided socialists, secularists and cowardly half-hearted "Christian sell-outs", becoming just another immoral, inconsequential, impotent shadow of the nation we once were?

The future of this great nation is up to you and me; please... don't desert her now. Remember, we are fighting the most important battle of our lives to see if we'll be successful in _**Restoring America's Soul!**_

ABOUT THE AUTHOR

My name is L T Nielsen. I'm a builder, an author and an artist. I was born in 1950 and raised by a father who was a Drill Sergeant during WWII. Perhaps that explains my practical no-nonsense approach to life.

I studied art, but also served six years in the Air National Guard, and believe every young man should be required by law to serve in one of the five branches of the military for a period of at least one year during their lifetime. (Prior to age 30) During that time, they should be required to learn the History of the U.S. Military as well as the *real* history of the United States. (Not the watered-down rewrites of liberal educators who want to change history and denigrate this country.)

I'm a true Christian, whose pragmatic approach to life and morality, coupled with a burning testimony of Christ as the God of all creation *requires* me to take a stand for truth and right. And I encourage others to join with me in an effort to rescue this nation from the forces of evil that are trying to destroy it on every front.

I'm a believer in the **original teachings of Jesus Christ,** and dismiss the notion that Christ's teachings are antiquated or outdated. I believe that only by living the precepts Christ taught over 2000 years ago, and following **to the letter** the things he taught as Gospel will we be able to inherit one of the mansions he said his Father had prepared for those who remained faithful to his teachings.

I reject the liberal idea that Christ doesn't actually *expect* us to obey all of his commandments. Why did he give them if he didn't expect us to live them? And I believe that much of the unhappiness and unrest in the world today would be eliminated if we'd simply follow his teachings and do the things he's asked us to do.

Conservative Christians understand that the things we do in life are actually important preparations for REAL life... that life which begins *after* death and resurrection where we will dwell with Christ forever.

Liberals on the other hand embrace the short-sighted myopic view that life is simply for their own personal pleasure... and that nothing we do in life really matters in the eternities. This arrogant view will come back to bite them in the end.

I also believe our nation is in deep trouble, and that the *traditional* family, **the fundamental building block of society** is in danger of being destroyed and replaced by a perverted liberal view of "families" that could prove to be the absolute destruction of America and Christianity as we know it. ***Something must be done to save our families and our nation NOW!***

Please... join with me. And together we *can* make a difference in the direction and the destiny of this, the greatest nation on God's Earth!